THE POWER OF REPARATION

RAOUL PLUS, S. J.

The POWER of Reparation

Steps to Restoring a Fallen World

SOPHIA INSTITUTE PRESS
Manchester, New Hampshire

Copyright © 2024

The Power of Reparation was first published in 1921 as *The Ideal of Reparation* (London: Burns, Oates, and Washbourne, Ltd.). The present edition includes only minimal formatting and typographical changes that do not affect the original content or style. Citations have been added or amended where necessary.

Printed in the United States of America. All rights reserved.

Cover by LUCAS Art & Design, Jenison, MI

Cover image: *The Crucifixion with the Virgin and Saint John* by Agnolo di Taddeo Gaddi

Bible quotations are from the Challoner version of the Douay-Rheims Bible per the imprint of John Murphy Company (Baltimore, 1899), excepting those marked with an asterisk (*) — these indicate the author's original translation from the Latin Vulgate.

No part of this book may be reproduced, stored in a retrieval system, or transmitted in any form, or by any means, electronic, mechanical, photocopying, or otherwise, without the prior written permission of the publisher, except by a reviewer, who may quote brief passages in a review.

Approbations from the original:

NIHIL OBSTAT: F. Thomas Bergh, O.S.B., Censor Deputatus.

IMPRIMATUR: Edm. Can. Surmont, Vicarius Generalis.

Westminster, September 1, 1921

Sophia Institute Press
Box 5284, Manchester, NH 03108
1-800-888-9344
www.SophiaInstitute.com

Sophia Institute Press is a registered trademark of Sophia Institute.

paperback ISBN 979-8-88911-054-5

ebook ISBN 979-8-88911-055-2

Library of Congress Control Number: 2024936654

First printing

NIHIL OBSTAT:
F. THOMAS BERGH, O.S.B.,
Censor Deputatus.

IMPRIMATUR:
EDM. CAN. SURMONT,
Vicarius Generalis.

WESTMONASTERII,
Die 1 *Septembris,* 1921.

Contents

Scripture Citation Abbreviations. viii
Publisher's Preface ix
Author's Preface: Who Will Make Reparation? xi
Introduction: In What Reparation Consists 3
Part I: Why Reparation Should Be Made 5
    Chapter 1: Reparation Is a Fundamental Obligation of
        Christianity 7
    Chapter 2: Our Lord Wishes Us to Make Reparation. 19
    Chapter 3: Reparation, an Actual Demand of Today 31
Part II: Who Should Make Reparation 45
    Chapter 4: Christians and Reparation. 47
    Chapter 5: Religious and Reparation 63
    Chapter 6: Priests and Reparation. 77
Part III: How Reparation Should Be Made 97
    Preliminary Note 99
    Chapter 7: How We Can Make Reparation by Leading
        a Simple Christian Life 101
    Chapter 8: How Religious Can Make Reparation. 117
Conclusion. 139
Appendix A: Prayers for Making Reparation. 145
Appendix B: Encyclical On Reparation 179
Solemn Act of Reparation 201
About the Author 205
Endnotes. 207

Scripture Citation Abbreviations

Abbr	Full	Abbr	Full
1 Cor	1 Corinthians	Ez	Ezechiel (Ezekiel)
1 Esd	1 Esdras (Ezra)	Gal	Galatians
1 Jn	1 John	Gn	Genesis
1 Kgs	1 Kings (1 Samuel)	Hb	Habacuc (Habakkuk)
1 Mc	1 Machabees	Heb	Hebrews
1 Par	1 Paralipomenon (1 Chronicles)	Is	Isaias (Isaiah)
1 Pt	1 Peter	Jas	James
1 Thes	1 Thessalonians	Jer	Jeremias (Jeremiah)
1 Tm	1 Timothy	Jb	Job
2 Cor	2 Corinthians	Jl	Joel
2 Esd	2 Esdras (Nehemiah)	Jn	John (Gospel)
2 Jn	2 John	Jon	Jonas (Jonah)
2 Kgs	2 Kings (2 Samuel)	Jo	Josue (Joshua)
2 Mc	2 Machabees	Jude	Jude
2 Par	2 Paralipomenon (2 Chronicles)	Jgs	Judges
2 Pt	2 Peter	Jdt	Judith
2 Thes	2 Thessalonians	Lam	Lamentations
2 Tm	2 Timothy	Lv	Leviticus
3 Jn	3 John	Lk	Luke
3 Kgs	3 Kings (1 Kings)	Mal	Malachias (Malachi)
4 Kgs	4 Kings (2 Kings)	Mk	Mark
Abd	Abdias (Obadiah)	Mt	Matthew
Acts	Acts of the Apostles	Mi	Micheas (Micah)
Agg	Aggeus (Haggai)	Na	Nahum
Am	Amos	Nm	Numbers
Apoc	Apocalypse (Revelation)	Os	Osee (Hosea)
Bar	Baruch	Phlm	Philemon
Cant	Canticle of Canticles (Song of Songs)	Phil	Philippians
		Prv	Proverbs
Col	Colossians	Ps	Psalms
Dn	Daniel	Rom	Romans
Dt	Deuteronomy	Ru	Ruth
Eccles	Ecclesiastes	Soph	Sophonias (Zephaniah)
Ecclus	Ecclesiasticus (Sirach)	Ti	Titus
Eph	Ephesians	Tb	Tobias (Tobit)
Est	Esther	Ws	Wisdom
Ex	Exodus	Zac	Zacharias (Zechariah)

Publisher's Preface

FIRST PUBLISHED IN ENGLISH as *The Ideal of Reparation* in 1921 (London: Burns, Oates, and Washbourne, Ltd.), this little work of doctrine and devotion was conceived by the renowned French Jesuit Fr. Raoul Plus as a means of disabusing the Christian faithful of a false notion of "Christianity without the Cross." The author describes the problem succinctly:

> Too few of the faithful have the faintest conception of the Christian life. ... Briefly stated, they believe in an easy-going, comfortable kind of Christianity destined for the majority of Christians, whereas the other kind of Christianity, austere and crucifying, is reserved for those stern characters or fantastical people who feel drawn to it.

As the author further explains, the spiritual work of reparation remains forever normative for the Christian life, and essential to any growth in spiritual perfection.

Although Catholics of the early 1900s would respond with generosity to such correctives from their spiritual shepherds—particularly following the celebrated papal encyclical on reparation, *Miserentissimus Redemptor* (Pius XI, 1928)—the very notion of reparation would almost entirely vanish from the Catholic mindset in the span of two generations, as sweeping liturgical changes in the 1960s and 1970s witnessed the doctrine's systematic removal from newly created rites of Mass, the Sacraments, and other blessings. The present work therefore offers a timely reminder for souls endeavoring to respond to the universal call to holiness.

For this new edition entitled *The Power of Reparation*, only the most careful adjustments have been made to the original text. The first is that all citations (excepting Scripture references) have been relocated to endnotes for greater readability. The few changes made to the body text include an update to the typography and capitalization standard, and the removal of one sentence appropriate to the original French audience—all in the interest of making the text more suitable for a universal readership. Finally, two appendices have been added: The first consists of prayers of reparation from various classic works, including the 1898 edition of the *Raccolta* and the famous Baltimore prayer book; the second is an English translation of *Miserentissimus Redemptor* that would reward private study as well as group discussion.

We are pleased to share the wisdom and spiritual insight of Fr. Raoul Plus with another generation, recalling everyone to the much-needed practice of reparation in the Christian life.

AUTHOR'S PREFACE

WHO WILL MAKE REPARATION?

THESE PAGES ARE DEDICATED to those Christians whose eyes are open and who have a heart, to these alone and to no others. Those who are not resolved to be generous with God need read no further.

This book is dedicated to those who have seen Christ crucified, the Church crucified, France crucified. It is not for those who have seen nothing of this triple crucifixion — apparently, such are to be found.

It is for those who, gazing upon this picture of death, have realized the necessity of some work of life; not for those who have gazed upon the dead body of their Lord, upon millions of the slain, mere lifeless bodies, without a moment's reflection, without a feeling of indignation prompting them, like Elias of old, to exclaim: *Quid hic agis, Elia?* — "What dost thou here, Elias? In the midst of these ruins, dost thou remain listless, indifferent, inactive?" *Et vos hic sedebitis?* (see 3 Kgs 19:9, 13; Nm 32:6).

In his *Journal of a Convert*, Van der Meer de Walcheren gives an account of a "Revival Meeting" in London. Two ministers came from America; they hired the Albert Hall, where they addressed more than fifteen thousand men. One of these preachers invited all who desired to give themselves to God to come forward. Clearly his voice rang out: "Who will come to the Lord?" For some time, the immense audience remained in anxious, impressive silence. Then one voice was raised: "I will." At once, from all parts that cry "I will," "I will," reechoed. And while the people were slowly coming down the long flights of stairs and making their way to the front benches, the two missionaries, stretching out their arms to them, continued their exhortation: "Who will come to the Lord?" Thousands responded and the cry "I will" resounded continually throughout the hall.

We do not need these emotional scenes, more or less artificial. It suffices for us to remember the words of Christ: *Si quis vult venire*—"If any man will ..." (Mt 16:24). We need volunteers, souls that offer themselves willingly and that are faithful to their engagements.

Lord Jesus, raise up these volunteers, souls that rightly understand the Christian life, and likewise the nature and necessity of reparation, volunteers whose nobility of soul leads them to give themselves wholly according to their state of life. Already there are many such, but the number must be doubled, trebled, nay increased tenfold. The world will be saved when we have a sufficient number of souls devoted to reparation and not before.

Will anyone offer himself? Many devote their energies to objects far less noble, but none offers such hidden glory, such imperative urgency as reparation.

Si quis vult venire—"If any man will …" Who is willing?

Here am I, Lord, *I will*. Enlighten and strengthen me. Already, I am won over to Thy cause. Lord, I will.

THE POWER OF REPARATION

Introduction

IN WHAT REPARATION CONSISTS

TO *REPAIR* MEANS TO put a thing in good condition again. When a house becomes dilapidated and uninhabitable, it has to be repaired or *restored*. Sometimes the damage utterly destroys an object. In this case, reparation means *compensation*, giving the equivalent.

In the moral sphere, the equivalent, the ransom for injury sustained, can only be given by the oblation of one's self. No material object can adequately compensate. How can order be reestablished? By some penalty inflicted upon the wrongdoer or self-imposed. Having allowed himself an unlawful and unbridled pleasure, it is just that some pain, duly proportioned, should reestablish the moral equilibrium. This is self-evident, without our discussing theories arising from the problem of God's vindictive justice. In this case, the equivalent of the wrong done is called expiation and, as in the preceding examples, can be offered by the guilty party himself, or by one, guiltless of the crime, who offers himself as surety.

In this book and in the Christian meaning of the verb, *to repair* has a triple signification: *restore, compensate, expiate*. Having once stated these facts, we will now briefly explain:

    I.   *Why* reparation should be made.

   II.   *Who* ought to make it.

  III.   *How* it should be made.

PART I

WHY REPARATION SHOULD BE MADE

BECAUSE IT IS:

1. *A fundamental obligation of Christianity.*
2. *The formal wish of our Lord.*
3. *An imperative necessity, given the circumstances.*

Chapter 1

Reparation Is a Fundamental Obligation of Christianity

Why did Christ come upon earth? To make reparation; for no other reason. He came to repair His divine work which sin had ruined, to restore to man his supernatural life; to compensate, by His merits, for the insult offered to the Father in the Garden of Eden and for those insults which man's malice daily renews and multiplies. He came to expiate by His sufferings — in the stable, during His hidden life, and on the Cross — the human selfishness which began with man's creation and never ceases.

Our dear Lord could have performed this work of reparation alone, but He did not so will it. He has chosen as associates each one of us, every Christian. We must grasp this truth well, for it is the foundation of the doctrine of reparation.

St. Paul, when speaking to the early Christians of their preeminent dignity of sharing the very life of the Son of

God, tells them that as Jesus lives by the Father, so they live by Jesus; He shares that life in virtue of His divine nature, they in virtue of their adoption. He is their Head; they are the living members, who, in virtue of His sacrifice, possess a divine life. They are "divinely naturalized." Union is only perfect when the members are united to the head and the head to the members. The Person of Christ is the Head, they are His members, His Mystical Body.

Hence, according to the teaching of our Lord—"I am the Vine, you are the branches" (Jn 15:5)—and that of St. Paul, the Catholic Church teaches that the *personal* Christ, consisting of the union of His divine and human nature, such as, of old, He lived in Bethlehem, Nazareth, and Jerusalem, such as He now lives in the Holy Eucharist, such as He lives and will live in heaven until the end of time, does not constitute the *whole* Christ. He has willed it thus. The *whole* Christ consists of Himself—the Head, *plus* ourselves, His Mystical Body. Our intimate union with His life explains why our Lord has associated us so closely with His work of Redemption.

Yet, as we have said, our Savior could have perfectly accomplished it alone. He does not need us to add to His merits, but He wills to make use of us, that He may increase ours. He is *the* Christ; we Christians are each of us *alter Christus*—"another Christ." We must work together. The Redemption will only be brought about by the will of our Savior—the first Christ, and of all Christians, those *other* Christs. Undoubtedly, His participation and ours differ immeasurably. His has an intrinsic, infinite value and is, of itself, infinitely sufficient. God could have dispensed with our cooperation, but because He loves us, He asks for it.

At the Offertory of the Holy Mass, the priest first puts wine in the chalice. Then, under pain of mortal sin, he has to add a few drops of water. Thus, our Lord's role and ours are symbolized, together with the proportional value of His action and ours. The wine alone would suffice for the validity of the Consecration. Nevertheless, the drops of water must be added, and by the effect of the divine words of Consecration, they are changed, as well as the wine, into the Precious Blood.

Granted, our part in the Redemption of the world is infinitesimally small; what are a few drops of water? But God requires it and He transubstantiates this tiny addition by uniting it with His own offering. This mere nothing becomes all-powerful, in virtue of the power communicated to it by God.[1] Thanks to this "nothing" which has become "something," souls will be ransomed. Without the offering of this "nothing" — so intrinsically insignificant and yet so really precious, on account of our union with Christ — many souls would probably be lost. The world needs all its potential saviors: it needs Jesus, its chief Savior, its Savior *par excellence*; it needs each one of us, who are called to cooperate with Him in the Redemption of the world. As Lacordaire says: "The human race had perished as a whole, by men's solidarity, that is to say, by its corporeal and moral union with Adam, its origin. Hence, it was fitting that humanity should be saved in the measure and manner of its loss, that is, by the means of solidarity. Where the solidarity of evil had lost all, by the solidarity of good, all has been reestablished."[2]

We are almost ignorant of our greatness as Christians, if we do not know our obligation of sharing in the work of Redemption. If we try to shirk our part, we are omitting a most noble, as well as a most peremptory, duty.

But we must examine this matter more closely. *How* did Christ make reparation?

By suffering.

Here a problem confronts us. The Son of God, desiring to renew His work, to restore all to its primitive condition, *instaurare omnia* (Eph 1:10), was not obliged to choose a plan of redemption which would involve for Himself a life of suffering, pain, and humiliation. Yet it was precisely this plan that He chose, rejecting all others, because He willed to repair all by suffering.

Whence it follows that, as we are necessarily united with Christ in His mission, since we form His Mystical Body, so we must necessarily cooperate with Him in His sufferings or "Passion." Therefore, St. Paul, when explaining the necessity of our cooperating with Jesus in His work of Redemption, goes straight to the point and tells us that we must "fill up those things that are wanting," not in the *mission* of Christ, but in His *Passion* (*Adimpleo ea quæ desunt passionem Christi.* — Col 1:24). The two unite, neither can exist alone. We must make reparation with Christ, and we can only do this by uniting our sacrifice with His.

Bossuet writes: "In order to become the Savior of men, Jesus Christ willed to be a Victim. But since He has a Mystical

Body, it follows that if the Head is immolated, all the members likewise must become living victims."[3]

Here is the progression — we might more correctly say, the equation — be a Christian, a savior, a victim.

Nor is the term *victim* something strange or new. This doctrine is as old as the gospel. It is the very foundation of the preaching of St. Paul, of the early Fathers, and of the Church in all ages. The apostle, in his Letter to the Romans, sets forth this doctrine very clearly. He writes: "I beseech you therefore, brethren, by the mercy of God, *that you present your bodies a living sacrifice, holy, pleasing unto God*" (12:1).

We cannot be true Christians and at the same time strive to lead a comfortable life, hoping at its close to pass quietly, without any shock, from a world in which we were very well off, to a heaven where we shall be perfectly happy; a heaven that is to be the reward of a life in which practically our chief anxiety has been to leave to others the laborious task of cooperating with Christ in redeeming the world. No, indeed, such a program is incompatible with the gospel of our divine Master. His program is totally different; it consists in the "terrible seriousness of human life," as Bossuet calls it.

Van der Meer de Walcheren, in the introduction to his *Journal of a Convert* — mentioned in our preface — speaking with his usual bitterness, which is for once fully justified, says: "I am well aware that there are many so-called rational animals, who seem to live sixty or eighty years and are some day buried without ever once emerging from their nothingness. ... Appearances were enough for them, all else had no existence." "Happily," he adds, "there are some real men, some who are really alive, and who have not received their souls in vain."

Shortly before his conversion, he says, referring to the same subject: "I am more and more stupefied at seeing the majority of men living on so calmly, not troubling themselves in the least about anything whatever. They wear a fat, self-satisfied smile, never giving a thought to *the yawning depths about us.*"

Yes, deep abysses surround us: that of man's sin, that of God's love. God has placed the latter close to the former, and we stand between the two with our role clearly and imperatively defined. It is characteristic of the true disciple of Jesus Christ that he has found out these abysses and, in consequence, lives in an irrepressible anxiety for the salvation of the world, both on account of the sterility of the Precious Blood and of his share of responsibility in the story of the divine life upon earth.

All Christians are under two obligations: First, they *must make reparation* in union with Jesus Christ, Who came upon earth solely for this purpose and, with Whom, they form one unit. Secondly, they must make this reparation *as He wills* — namely, *by suffering.*

Too few of the faithful have the faintest conception of the Christian life; they seem to imagine that practically there are two doctrines taught by our Lord, or at least two ways of interpreting His one law — one consisting in trying to suffer, the other in striving not to suffer at all; one of deliberate mortification, the other of deliberate avoidance of whatever is irksome. Briefly stated, they believe in an easy-going, comfortable kind of Christianity destined for the majority of Christians, whereas the other kind of Christianity, austere and crucifying, is reserved for those stern characters or fantastical people who feel drawn to it.

They find it quite natural that a priest, such as the Curé d'Ars, a saint, should write as follows: "Everything reminds us of the Cross. We ourselves are made in the form of a cross. Balm and sweetness exhale from the Cross. The unction, which overflows from the Cross, inundates our souls, in proportion as we unite ourselves with it, holding it tightly against our hearts. The Cross contains more wisdom than any book; all who do not know this book are ignorant, however many other books they may have studied. Those only are truly wise who love and consult this book, who study it deeply. Bitter as this book is, they are never happier than when they can immerse themselves in its bitterness. The more they frequent this school, the more they desire to remain there, never do their studies weary them."

In a novitiate of the Franciscans of Mary, in Canada, on one occasion, six religious were wanted to go to China to take care of some lepers. There were forty novices, and all the forty volunteered, each eager to have that honor. Some Christians, hearing this, remark coldly: "It is their vocation." The very examples which should arouse these lax souls and convince them that they are bound to do something, if not as much as these nuns, only serve as specious pretexts for justifying their inaction.

They argue thus: "Monks and nuns remain in prayer all night, prostrate before the altar, or rise for prayer at two in the morning in order that we may sleep on comfortably in a good bed. They pass their time in prayer in order to dispense us from this exceedingly disagreeable task. They deprive themselves of food, therefore we can allow ourselves every luxury. They live in whitewashed cells, furnished only, like those of Carmelites, with a crucifix, a holy water stoup, a death's head, and a discipline, so that we may adorn our houses with numerous ornaments and every modern comfort. If these religious go without fires, it is to allow us to have an excellent system of heating and a pleasant temperature in our rooms and passages. They sleep on a plank or a straw mattress, that we may have silken eiderdown coverlets and embroidered counterpanes. Their only jewelry is the cross, therefore we can wear trinkets and pearl necklaces that cost a fortune."

Undoubtedly, the perfect life exacts an amount of suffering, for which an ordinary Christian life does not call, but can we imagine any truly enlightened Christian life — even an ordinary one — that in any way harmonizes with the feverish and pagan pursuit of the comforts of life, which modern materialism tries — and, unhappily, too often with success — to impose upon so many of Christ's disciples?

What then! Is Christ, perchance, divided? — *Nonne divisus est Christus?* (1 Cor 1:13). Are there two Christs? Is there a Crucified Christ, whom we can only serve by our crucifixion, and a restful Christ, whom we can manage to follow quite well while partaking of all life's joys and pleasures? St. Paul did not preach two Christs. He knew of One only, "Christ Crucified" — *Christum et hunc crucifixum* (1 Cor 2:2).

Men have changed this since St. Paul's time. Now they know of two. The first, the true Christ, did not suffice, so they invented another, one without a cross, or a crucifying doctrine, a Christ without those two beams which cast such a disquieting impressive shadow, a Christ whose demands amount to this: Live as you please; I promise you a happy eternity, provided that "you turn to Me in your last moments with your darkening mind, that you repent with your failing will and give Me the alms of your last breath."[4]

There is no such Christ as this for Christians who will not suffer. The disciple is not greater than his Master. Our Savior has suffered, and every Christian must suffer in some form or other — as we shall explain — if he would not prove false to his name, or fail to accomplish his mission; he must always and necessarily be the friend of suffering.

A great Belgian statesman took for his motto: "Rest elsewhere." The day of perfect happiness, perhaps not far off, will surely dawn, perhaps soon, and will have no sunset. Meanwhile, time is given us that we may merit "the joy of the Lord." *Intra in gaudium Domini tui* (Mt 25:21, 23). But we can only enter into the joy of the Lord on condition that upon earth we have shared the sufferings of our Lord. Christ was the first to choose suffering as the way into glory. "Golgotha is not a rhetorical flourish." For us too the same rule holds — *oportuit pati Christum, et ita intrare in gloriam suam* (Lk 24:26).

We wish to triumph with Him, therefore we must fight with Him. In the *Exercises* of St. Ignatius, in the "Contemplation on the Kingdom," the saint places these words on our Lord's lips: *Laborare mecum.* Pizarro, a conqueror of South America, disembarked and threw his sword upon the ground to mark off the bravest, and called out: "Let all who are afraid remain where they are, let the others cross over and follow me."

This is stern language, and, in spite of the convincing force of the doctrine, many draw back rather than face the suffering which is the inevitable consecration of all Christian life.

"How those two arms of the Cross frighten me, as they stand out on the hill of Calvary! I feel more inclined to hide behind them than to be nailed upon them!"

"Yes, the wood is hard; but there is something more than the wood. There is One nailed to those arms. The wood is dead, but a living One is fastened to it. Looking at the Cross, as we ought to look at it, we no longer see the two arms, they disappear or at least become indistinct; the body hanging there, alone rivets our attention and, in the midst of this body, shining through an open wound — the Heart. We say: 'The crucifix.' We are wrong: for we appear to name a *thing*. We ought to say: 'The Crucified,' for that shows a person."

"A person? Yes, in truth, a Person Who is both human and divine. What! Is it Thou, my God, Who hangest there?"

"Yes, it is I."

"Now I seem to understand better, I almost grasp the truth: I will suffer with Thee, Lord, but Thou wilt suffer with me. With Thee, I shall be brave and march resolutely forward."

"That thou mayest have still more courage, stand at the foot of My Cross and look round upon the world. Look at

My executioners as they go down the slope of Calvary; look at Jerusalem, wrapped in slumber, where the multitudes know nothing. Thou must suffer in order that My Redemption may avail them. I have willed that thou shouldst help Me. I can do all with thee and nothing without thy aid. Wilt thou that we save the world together? Or dost thou prefer to go away along with all the crowd?"

"Art Thou really speaking to me, Lord? Surely, Thou knowest not who I am!"

"Thou art one of Mine own. Is that not enough for Me to ask thee to work, suffer, and endure with Me? The task is immense as thou seest. But I assure thee that it is worth the price, though it involve the oblation of thyself as a living victim, in union with Me, even in thy present state of life."

"Dost Thou think I can? A living victim along with Thee, O Lord? Ah, yes, with all my heart—take me!"

CHAPTER 2

Our Lord Wishes Us to Make Reparation

THE NECESSITY FOR OUR making reparation is logically deduced from the very foundation of our Catholic Faith and, in particular, from the doctrine of the Mystical Body of Christ, and that of the Redemption. It is likewise shown to be an imperative duty from the long, formal, and constantly reiterated chain of instructions given by our Blessed Lord.

Whether we open the Gospels, or examine the great revelations handed down to us, we constantly see our Lord setting forth His great desire to find souls capable of suffering, utilizing it for the glory of God and the salvation of souls.

Let us turn first to the Gospel. There are numerous texts which teach the obligation of doing penance as an act of reparation; no law is more frequently inculcated.

Our Master chose St. John the Baptist as His precursor. What did he preach? "The baptism of penance for the remission of sins" (Lk 3:3). What does he continually repeat, day after day, on the banks of the Jordan, where Jesus Himself was soon to commence His ministry? "Do penance, for the Kingdom of heaven is at hand" (Mt 3:2). How does he live? As an example: "John had his garment of camel's hair, ... his meat was locusts and wild honey," his abode "the desert of Judea" (Mt 3:4, 1). How does he answer those who came to him asking: "Who art thou?" — "I am the voice of one crying in the wilderness: Make straight the way of the Lord" (Jn 1:22, 23). Men had made God's path crooked; it had to be made straight again: this is reparation.

What a well-merited rebuke he gave to those hypocrites who came to ask for the baptism of penance, without any intention or desire to lead a better life! "Ye brood of vipers. ... Bring forth fruit worthy of penance. ... The axe is laid to the root of the trees. Every tree that doth not yield good fruit shall be cut down and cast into the fire. ... Hasten, for there cometh One; He is even now among you, and you know Him not. If He finds good wheat, He will gather it into His barns, but He will burn up the chaff with unquenchable fire" (see Mt 3:7–12; Jn 1:26).

Is it possible to set forth, in a clearer or more thrilling manner, the necessity of suffering as an act of expiation, the obligation of returning to the straight path, of atoning for past faults, of imploring pardon by offering some proportionate penance?

Afterward, our Blessed Lord Himself appeared in public. He commenced His ministry by fasting in the desert for forty days. When He called men to be His apostles, He bade them leave all and follow Him, and exhorted the crowds that surrounded Him to deny themselves. St. Matthew significantly remarks: "From that time, Jesus began to preach and to say: Do penance, for the Kingdom of heaven is at hand" (4:17). St. Matthew seems to point out that from the very beginning of Jesus' public life, He preached on the theme so dear to Him and so constantly reiterated in His discourses.

Moreover, our Lord extolled suffering and expiation for sin all His life. He taught men to give one coat to the poor if they had two; not to trouble about what they should wear; that money was to be despised and heavenly treasures alone valued. He constantly anathematized those who loved the broad road, and ever strove to lead men to walk in the narrow way. He predicted untold woes to the rich and to hypocrites. He taught men that the truly blessed are those who are poor and gentle; those who weep; those who thirst for justice, who are merciful, pure in heart; those who are peacemakers, and who suffer persecution. Such is His doctrine! "Are you willing," He asks, "to follow Me seriously? Then, as a preliminary step, you must deny yourselves and embrace the cross with both hands: nothing less will avail."

Our Lord does not restrict His teaching to words: had God merely given maxims or precepts, He would not have been understood. He reduced His words to actions: "The Word was made flesh" (Jn 1:14). That which had hitherto reached only to the ear became visible to the eye: precept became example. Jesus lived His whole life upon earth as a Victim, that He might give us an example and teach us how to suffer.

As soon as He came into this world—*ingrediens mundum*—how did He explain His life's work? *Dicit: Hostiam et oblationem noluisti. ... Tunc dixi: Ecce venio* ("He saith: The victims of the past thou wouldest not. ... Then said I: Behold, I come" — Heb 10:5, 7*).

In the womb of Mary, Jesus only began His apprenticeship for the victim's life He was to lead later on in the confinement of innumerable tabernacles. Jesus was born; and in the manger, in the stable, in Bethlehem, He was still a Victim. As Tertullian writes: "He was a Victim from the virgin birth." From His birth onward, His sufferings continued; He endured the circumcision, the flight into Egypt, the exile there — nothing was lacking as regards suffering. Hence, in His public life, Jesus could say: "Blessed are those that suffer. Blessed are the poor" (Mt 5:10; Lk 6:20). How these words would have provoked resentment, had He been born in luxury! But He was the most destitute and afflicted of all.

In Nazareth, He lived a hidden life. Had He not done so, men would never have accepted the doctrine of humility which He preached afterward. As it is, in spite of His example, how few trouble about His doctrine! Men love to be seen; He effaced Himself during thirty years. A ransom was required to atone for men's pride, so Jesus lived a hidden, obscure life of painful toil. Holman Hunt, in his celebrated painting "The Shadow of the Cross," represents our Lord stopping work, standing up, and stretching out his arms to ease their weariness. The light flings His shadow back upon the blank wall, which is horizontally divided by a shelf from which hang some carpenter's tools. The effect is striking. It is that of a man's form standing out in relief from a cross.

During His public life, Jesus, wearied and footsore, tramped the roads of Palestine in search of souls. He was thirsty and asked the woman of Samaria for a drink; He spent nights in prayer; unceasingly He exercised His ministry. Foxes have their holes; birds, their nests; but the Son of Man had not where to lay His head, not a roof to shelter Him. He had to make reparation for all those who pursue vain things, and worship the golden calf; for the children of God who either forget or deliberately neglect to pray to Him; for the sowers of evil seeds, and for those in whom the good seed remains sterile. When Jesus began His ministry, what name did the Baptist give Him? "The Lamb of God ... Who taketh away the sin of the world" (Jn 1:29). John meant: "Here is the silent Victim for all men Who will save the world." Throughout three years, Jesus, with divine patience, endeavored to impress upon His apostles that the Christ must be delivered up to His enemies. They could not understand His words; their meaning only dawned upon them when, from their hiding places in Jerusalem, they saw Him afar off nailed to the Cross on the summit of Calvary.

But above all, Jesus stands forth as our Victim in His Passion. Then, because He so willed, He was betrayed, denied, insulted, buffeted, outraged, and nailed to the Cross. Thus He willed to teach us to suffer in our body, our affections, our reputation, and our honor. He suffered likewise, because divine justice required some compensation for all those who only live for pleasure, who betray their baptismal vows and their Faith, for those who deny the Faith, who mock at the Passion and persecute Christ's disciples, for those who scoff at the Church, the pope, and priests—in a word, for all who, in their shameless egoism, find the Cross of Christ so irksome. Christ so much loved reparation that He glorified it in Mary Magdalene, once publicly known as a sinner, who became in "Mary of Bethania," where He called her to Himself, a model of repentance and love, and afterward Mary of Golgotha. At the foot of the Cross there were but three—you will never find many where there is suffering to endure—three only, one man and two women—Mary, John, and the Magdalene between two who had never lost their innocence, one with innocence regained at the price of generous expiation through a twofold breakage, her broken vase and her broken heart. To such a degree was her soul purified, that she was the first, after our Lady, who was privileged to see the Risen Savior on Easter morning.[5]

We have seen how greatly our Lord values reparation; leaving the Gospel, let us now turn to the great revelations handed down to us in the history of the Church. What do we learn from those of Paray, Lourdes, La Salette, Pellevoisin, Pontmain?

In the revelations made to St. Margaret Mary, our Lord's one object appears to have been to ask for reparatory sacrifices. Let us take a few examples from her life: On one occasion Jesus said to her: "Behold the Heart, which has so loved men and in return only receives ingratitude and contempt. That is why I ask thee to make reparation."

The saint tells us: "The Sacred Heart wills that souls should make reparation by returning Him love for love, and that they should humbly implore pardon of God for all the insults that are offered to Him."

Again, Jesus said to her: "My daughter, it is true that My Heart has sacrificed everything for men, without receiving from them any return. I feel this more acutely than the torments of My Passion. In spite of all My eagerness to do them good, they treat Me with coldness and contempt. Give Me the pleasure of making up for their ingratitude."

In 1669 in the month of February, at the time of the Carnival, St. Margaret Mary wrote to the Rev. Mother de Saumise: "The loving Heart of Jesus seems to make me this request, namely, that I would stay with Him, close to His Cross in these days, during which all rush madly after pleasure, and that by the bitterness, which He will make me taste, I should, in some measure, compensate for the bitterness with which sinners immolate His Sacred Heart. He wishes me to grieve unceasingly with Him to prevent sinners from filling up the measure of their guilt."[6]

In order that reparation might be made by devout souls, our Lord asked for a special feast to be instituted in honor of His Sacred Heart, for the Communion of reparation on the first Friday of each month, and at other times for this same object; and for the practice of the holy hour. Most of Christ's instructions to St. Margaret Mary tended to train her — and through her ourselves — in a spirit of reparation.

This is what He asked of her for the holy hour: "Every week from the Thursday night to the Friday morning, I will cause thee to share in the deadly sadness which I allowed to overwhelm My soul in the Garden of Olives. Thou wilt rise between eleven o'clock and midnight and remain prostrate flat upon the ground for one hour, that thou mayest satisfy the divine justice, by imploring mercy for sinners and likewise, in some measure, mitigate the sadness I felt when My apostles abandoned Me and could not watch even one hour with Me."

It is impossible to misunderstand our Lord's meaning. The first time the Sacred Heart appeared to this saint, on December 27, 1673, He was seen upon the altar, the chosen place of sacrifice, with the face of one in pain. He asked her to draw a picture of His Sacred Heart, with the wound made by the lance, surrounded by a crown of thorns, and surmounted by a cross. Hence we can well understand the fiery utterances of St. Margaret Mary. She exclaims: "If only you knew how our Sovereign urges me to love Him with a love that will share His life of suffering! I know of nothing that is more fitted to ease the tiresomeness of our lives than patient endurance with love. Let us suffer lovingly without complaining and count as lost all moments passed without suffering." The whole life of this saint is one hymn of reparation, of love that begets conformity to His suffering life. It is useless to give copious citations from her Life or works, they must be read through.

The Rev. Père Terrien, in his well-grounded book on *Devotion to the Sacred Heart*, says: "To make reparation is to love, but above all to suffer, to sacrifice self through love."[7]

"It is in the Heart of Jesus that we obtain the precious supplement of love, which alone can render our reparations really pleasing to Him."

Jesus knocks at the door of our heart, asking us to make reparation, but our poor alms have no value unless they pass through His Heart. There is a blessed ebb and flow of the tide of love, it originates with Him and invites us, and our love must return to that center if we are to correspond effectually with His advances.

David said that he had found his heart that he might speak to God; we can do better than find ours, seeing that we have the Heart of the Son of God. St. Bonaventure's sole desire was to dwell therein. He pitied the blindness of those who do not know how to find entrance into Christ, through His open wounds, especially that of His Heart.

We then will say: *Introibo ad altare Dei*—"I will enter humbly, but resolutely, even to the altar of my God." In the Office of Lauds, the hymn for the feast of the Sacred Heart says in substance: "O Heart, Symbol of Christ's Passion of body and soul, as a Priest He offered in Thee His twofold sacrifice. Who would not venerate and love Thee? Who would not choose Thee for his dwelling place forever?" This holy sanctuary of His Heart, where Jesus continually renews His sacrifice, shall likewise be mine: there I will offer my humble share in His work of Redemption. How can I do this? By striving to unite my sentiments with those of His adorable Heart, in conformity with the spirit of the Apostleship of Prayer, which is one of many methods and ranks with the best.

But what are the sentiments of the Sacred Heart? Consider first His *Ecce venio!*—"Lo, I come, I offer, I give Myself." The whole life of Christ is one prolonged *Ecce*, one unceasing ratification of the immolation of His first day. *Ecce Rex!* on Palm Sunday. *Ecce Homo!* on Good Friday. *Ecce Agnus Dei!* There is our Lord on the banks of the Jordan and in the Eucharist. Mary, the most faithful of all His imitators, had her *Ecce* likewise. *Ecce ancilla!*—"I offer myself, I give myself up to Thee" was her unceasing prayer.

Two ardent desires continually flow from the Heart of Jesus. First, He is consumed by an insatiable thirst to do the will of His heavenly Father; secondly, He thirsts continually for the baptism of blood which is to save us from eternal death. Now this twofold desire extends, in Jesus, to all that constitutes Jesus.

It is indisputable that, in His personal humanity, our Blessed Lord can no longer humble Himself or suffer. But we constitute His Mystical Body, and He desires that each Christian should give himself wholly to the fulfilling of God's will. The Sacred Heart desires each one to offer those acts of reparation which have to be united to His own sacrifice. If Jesus can no longer humble Himself in Himself, He can do so in us, for we are one with Him. This is why He asks for our share and our offerings.

Alas, how few understand His appeal, how few accept! Nevertheless, all true devotion to the Sacred Heart goes as far as this. It even constitutes its very essence, and those who interpret it otherwise either diminish or distort it.

In the Eucharist, Jesus is with us under the form of the "Host," i.e., Victim, thus clearly expressing His ardent desires. Under the species of the Sacrament, our Lord does not actually suffer from the indifference, irreverence, immortification, pride, revolt, and sacrilege of men. But, when He trod this earth, He foresaw all these and suffered unspeakable tortures on account of these insults and outrages offered to the divine

Majesty and from man's horrible neglect of God's laws. He foresaw every single sinful act and atoned for each in detail.

He asks us to console Him now for all His Sacred Heart suffered in those hours of trial; He wills that, by our piety, we should make Him some compensation. Since He has chosen to perpetuate by the Holy Eucharist the sacrifice which He consummated upon the Cross, how can we better satisfy His desire than by continuing His sacrifice as He Himself does — i.e., by becoming victims in union with Him? And since, in this Sacrament of love, Jesus still mystically hungers unspeakably and suffers an unquenchable thirst to accomplish the will of God and save souls, what can we do better than enter into the sentiments of the divine Guest of our tabernacles?

We shall emphasize this point further on, when explaining the nature of the love for the Blessed Sacrament which should animate a soul devoted to reparation. Let what has been said suffice for the present. When we rightly understand true devotion to the Sacred Heart, our eucharistic life becomes the union of two hosts or victims in the union of one perfect oblation; and when we truly grasp the meaning of our eucharistic life, that is, of our union with Jesus as Victim, our devotion to the Sacred Heart then becomes practically one sustained effort of self-renunciation in order to become a living "appearance," under which Christ alone lives. We aim at becoming a living "appearance," that He may use us as an instrument to continue the accomplishment of His divine work; a living "appearance" that is unceasingly sacrificed with Him in the unity of the same sacrifice for the glory of the adorable Trinity and for the salvation of souls.

THE POWER OF REPARATION

We have dwelt somewhat on the revelations of Paray le Monial and the devotion to the Sacred Heart because they bear on the subject of reparation. This holds good of the great apparitions of our Lady in France — to mention only those of the nineteenth century. In all these it seems as though their sole object was to remind men of the need for reparation. To Bernadette, our Blessed Lady expressed her grief at the invasion and flooding of the world by sin, and as some compensation, she asked that men should pray and do penance. She told Bernadette to recite the Rosary and asked that a church should be built at Lourdes in which God would be glorified by the public homage of the ardent acclamations of countless pilgrims, boldly vindicating their living faith in an age characterized by blasphemy and forgetfulness of God. Above all, she insisted upon the necessity of doing penance, saying sorrowfully: "Penance, penance, penance."

When she appeared to two children at La Salette, she urged them to pray and do penance. She told them sorrowfully that God was about to chastise men severely unless they prayed and did penance. She mentioned blasphemy and the desecration of the Sabbath as the two sins that especially cried to heaven for vengeance.

What are we to learn from all this? The need of souls — souls devoted to reparation. God is saddened by men's sin. It will fare badly with us if there are not voluntary victims forthcoming to fling into the other scale of divine justice their sacrifices to God.

CHAPTER 3

Reparation, an Actual Demand of Today

THE MORE STERILE THE land, the greater is the call for labor. Morning and night we pray, "Thy Kingdom come," and yet what is more self-evident than the fact that our wish is still unrealized?

Who would dare assert that God's Kingdom has come? Is it not only too manifest that God's Kingdom has not come and that we see no signs whatever of its advent?

Péguy places on the lips of St. Joan of Arc some words which fittingly describe the sad state of things at the commencement of Charles VI's reign, words which can truthfully be said by us in our days: "Our Father, who art in heaven, how far, far off is the hallowing of Thy name, how far off the coming of Thy Kingdom! The world is worse than ever. If only we could see the Sun of Justice rise. But, O God, forgive me for venturing to say it, Thy Kingdom seems to be going farther and farther away. Never has Thy name been so blasphemed nor Thy will treated with such contempt. Never has man been so disobedient. We have not yet enough saints upon earth; send us as many as we need, as many as are necessary to dishearten the enemy."

Huysmans, in his admirable introduction to the Life of St. Lydwine of Schiedam (d. 1433), gives an outline of the state of the world when God chose Lydwine for Himself. When skating one day, she was knocked down and broke her ribs. Gangrene set in, and for thirty-eight years she endured intolerable sufferings both in soul and body. She was chosen by God to keep Satan thus in check, and to hinder the daily increase of his kingdom.

Has the world changed much since the times of St. Lydwine? In her days, men killed one another. Our age can vie with that of those older barbarians. Nations were crumbling to dust in decrepitude and decadence, men were willing bondslaves of paid sophists and false shepherds without a conscience. Have we not seen this also? Money to bribe traitors was plentiful in those times. Is it not always at hand? There are philosophers in abundance, now as then, ready to excuse the greatest atrocities.

Love of pleasure reigns universally. "In a few days, I shall be twenty-three. It is time to enjoy myself." This motto chosen by Beyle has been practically followed by whole generations. Sin displays itself with such disconcerting cynicism and abundance. One hardly knows where to stop when giving examples.

In an article entitled *Panem et circenses* (Bread and the show of the circus) — the cry of the populace of ancient

Rome—Monsieur Reverdy gives statistics of the amounts realized in 1915, the second year of the Great War, by the principal pleasure centers in France, such as theaters, cinemas, smoking concerts. The total amounted to 22,880,000 francs. Of this sum the theaters received 8,000,000 francs, the cinemas 7,000,000, and the concerts and music halls netted the rest. "Thus, nearly 23,000,000 francs (about £1,120,000 sterling) were spent on pleasure by a country in the throes of war, and in which few families had been spared bereavements in war victims. This is rather a large sum." "Large" indeed! It is neither more nor less than monstrous. Yet while our bishops and all who are zealous for the moral purity of our streets protest against the display of bad books and suggestive pictures, there are actually men who clamor for "room to be found for free and easy behavior and moving voluptuousness and even—why not?—for the indulged sensualism so often found in so many of our French literary masterpieces."

Then behind these open vices are all the faults that are sheltered and hidden.

"Lord, may Thy Kingdom come! Alas! How far off it still is!"

Out of 1,500,000,000 human beings, there are only 520,000,000 Christians: of this number, only 260,000,000 are Catholics, the rest are schismatics or Protestants. The remainder of the total consists of Jews, infidels, and pagans. Yet the dear Lord shed His blood for all!

Alas! We lack apostles. Twenty-seven centuries ago, the prophet Amos uttered this strange prophecy under the sycamores of Bethel: "Behold the days will come, saith the Lord, and I will send a famine into the land; not a famine of bread, not a thirst of water, but of hearing the word of the Lord. And they shall move from sea to sea, ... they shall go about seeking the word of the Lord and shall not find it" (8:11–12). It is the same now; although Christ has come, the nations sit in the shadow of death.

A tribe in Central Madagascar had been deprived of their pastor. He was needed elsewhere, for there was a dearth of priests. This is what the deserted flock wrote to his superior: "A terrible misfortune has happened to us. We are like men who have been suddenly plunged in utter darkness through the extinguishing of their torch. The torch of the Catholic Faith had shone upon us and made us supremely happy. Alas! How sad is our fate now! Help us, Father, hear our cry of distress; we are like sheep without a shepherd, the sport of wolves. Send us back our priest."

True devotedness to the cause that we espouse means a great deal. It entails the service of our mind and intelligence and above all of our heart. It means loving the cause we are eager to further so much, that we are prepared to sacrifice ourselves wholly together with our tastes, preferences, habits, and inclinations and not merely a given portion of them. It means loving souls so ardently that we go in pursuit of them, without waiting for them to come to us, without looking for their love and gratitude in return, but devoting ourselves solely for the love of God and of souls. Such self-devotedness is by no means easy, and this is why the world in desolation clamors for it. The source of divine grace is ever within reach, ready to gush forth in living streams and to cleanse men from sin, to purify conscience, give sight to the blind, heal the leper and the paralytic, but volunteers are needed, as at the Pool of Bethsaida, to bring God's help to succor the misery of humanity.

Valentine Riant used to say: "If devotedness is required, I am ready." She accepted generously the call to consecrate her life as one act of reparation for the abominations and vile crimes of the world. But how few have the courage to imitate her example!

After the siege of Paris in 1871, Rénan and some of his friends had a gold medal struck, bearing an inscription which ran thus: "During the war, some people used to meet at Brébant's every fortnight, and never once noticed that they were dining in a city numbering two millions of the besieged."

It is ever thus. The world contains two classes of people: the few who, like that generous victim of reparation, have eyes to see and intelligence to know what is passing around them, and who are so affected by the sight, that they are forced to give their assistance, and the others who, imitating Rénan, the egoist, and his associates—and their name is "legion"—see and understand nothing, or if they by chance obtain some inkling of the truth, take no heed. In the midst of a world that is hurrying on to destruction, they think only of feasting at the restaurants of their times. In any case, they give no thought to the millions of unhappy beings around them, creatures who are enslaved by wretchedness, doubts, and want of God. We all know Carlyle's caustic remark about the "Eighteen millions, *mostly fools*."

As we are so accustomed to live in the midst of egoism which prevails and rules everywhere, we do not perceive the hatefulness of this vice. Those whom some special grace has enlightened in their darkness of unbelief outside the Church, and led them suddenly to the clairvoyance of faith in the gospel, are full of astonishment and contempt for the "nobodies" who fill the world and want nothing beyond the vanities which satisfy their mean desires.

The Dutch artist, Pierre Van der Meer, in his *Journal*, owns that, while on his way to faith, he is amazed at seeing the utter indifference of some people, and they are the majority.

He passed through the city of London, "that mournful region of trade, money, and business. ... From every door, street, corner, by-place, and blind alley, gentlemen were dashing out, dressed in black and hatless. They all rushed in the same direction and apparently to the same place. A Japanese loan had just been floated, the subscription lists were open. Evidently, there was money to be won, and like savages they dashed after their prey."

Another time, he reached Paris by the express which arrived at 6 a.m. He writes: "On the Boulevards Rochechouart and Clichy, I witnessed the joys and sorrows of the preceding night. The chandeliers were still alight in a large room on the first floor of a café. Presently I heard the shrill harsh laugh of some girl. I met men and women in evening dress. With drawn tired features and dull eyes, they were hurrying home on foot or seeking for some conveyance."

Elsewhere, he sees men who simply live to eat. Speaking of one he says: "This glutton certainly has no fear of death, nor does he concern himself unduly with the mystery of life. What can be the life of the soul in such an individual?"

Again he writes: "An old American lady boards in our hotel." She boasts of having neither relatives nor friends. "Yet," she said, "all the same I have one unique friend; here it is," she added, as she threw down her purse on the table.

Consider two other examples of a worldly life. A young girl lay on her deathbed, and, just as she was expiring, she said to the nun who was nursing her: "Sister, my hands are empty."

An Austrian nobleman, a relative of Count Czernin, as he lay dying, said: "When God asks me to render an account of my life, what shall I answer? I can only say: Lord, I have killed hares and hares and hares, and nothing more. It is really too insignificant," and he spoke the truth. We are no partisans of Jansenism, no enemy of lawful amusements, but we condemn the terrible habit of looking at life from the sole point of view of how much pleasure it can be made to yield. There is something else to do.

But we have not yet touched bottom. Men might at least be contented with neglecting God, as is the case with the majority, but some go further. For them, it does not suffice to ignore God, they are animated by a most virulent hatred of their Creator and of the Catholic Church.

We were justly stirred up to anger and resentment by the sacrilegious fury of our enemies during the war against our churches; but was not a book entitled *The Great Tragedy of the Churches of France* published long before the war?

Yet, after all, material monuments are little compared with that great spiritual temple—the Catholic Church which is the Bride of Christ. How does the world treat it? We need not go far back in order to catch the echoes of menacing, inimical words in our public legislative assemblies.

Here are a few examples: "In 1905 or 1906 at the latest, Catholicism will be dead and buried." "I mean to put an end to this clerical reaction, three months will do. I need no more." "This is what you would say, O Catholic Church, but you no longer have any life in you." "The Church is falling to pieces." These sentiments were expressed as recently as 1903, 1904, 1906, and 1908.

Active measures followed upon these words, innumerable Acts against religion were passed. Thousands of the best disciples of Jesus Christ, torn between their patriotism and their Faith, had to go into exile. They alone know what great sacrifices this involved.

Look at that marble tablet placed over the entrance to a home for the aged. After the monks had left the Carthusian Monastery of Neuville, near Montreuil-sur-mer, the civil authorities made the building into an almshouse for the aged, and on this marble tablet in golden letters (well befitting the words, forsooth!) this inscription is inscribed:

"The sad and solitary life hitherto led in this cloistered monastery has disappeared forever. It has given place to a free and open life, active and fruitful for the progress of mankind. With the works of the past, we construct the works of the future."

This inscription is a quotation from the discourse delivered at the inauguration of the almshouse.

In France, we have had divorce laws, "priests turned into Tommies," and general laicization. Then came the laws of association, decrees to put us outside the law. And now we have Separation and the Inventories. And where is Jesus Christ in all this? And where are His teaching and His Vicar and His ministry, and His chosen disciples?

We yield to none in honoring our beloved country. But let us not imitate the pharisaism of those who refuse to acknowledge her mistakes. For the sake of her future let us make honest admissions.

Réné Bazin, writing during the war with his usual delicacy of expression, sets forth the anomaly of a crucifix — which for years had occupied a place of honor in the schoolroom — being found by some American soldiers in the schoolmistress's attic. The crucifix had been relegated to the rubbish heap! Surely such an act of vandalism helps to explain how a conversation such as the subjoined could take place. Two children were in the Museum at Cluny looking at a large crucifix: "Look, Madeleine," said one, "does not *that man* look wretched?" "Why does he hang down his head?" "He seems to be crying, don't you think so?"

Yes, poor little ones, indeed He weeps; He weeps because you do not know Him. He sheds tears because some of your own family have prevented your knowing and loving Him.

What meanness there is in these attacks against religion, be they open or secret! Formerly our coins bore the inscription: "God protects France." This glorious sentence has been suppressed, and it is considered a disgrace to name the Master of the universe in a public speech or an official document.

God! Why He no longer exists! One public statesman has grandiosely declared that "all the stars are extinguished." Another speaks of himself as "God's personal enemy." Jaurès, the greatest advocate of laicization, in an eloquent discourse that concealed assertions no less blasphemous, made the subjoined statements in the Chamber of Deputies on February 11, 1895:

"We must before all safeguard the priceless treasures acquired by man in spite of so many prejudices, sufferings, and combats. These treasures consist in the realization of certain principles, namely, that there is no such thing as revealed or sacred truth; that all truth which does not spring from man is but error; that even when we give our adhesion to certain principles, our critical faculty must always be on the alert. Further, that a certain aggressive mental attitude should underlie all that we think and affirm, that even though our ideal of God should take shape or if God were to manifest Himself to men under a tangible form, our first duty would be to refuse Him our obedience, to treat Him as an equal with Whom we discuss, not as a Master to Whom we submit."

And God sees all that: He hears all that! For whom do they take God? In vain do men assert that God is nothing, in vain do they stand forth and shake their fists at the sun and declare: "You don't exist." The sun still shines in the heavens, and God still counts.

Vile, degraded men who insult God and deny His very existence, who leave Him on one side, are powerless to injure the Most High. Those who deny and insult must remain here below. Heaven is inaccessible to them. Earth, alas! is not and are we sure that these insults rising from our midst will not fall back in punishments upon us?

God is God; all those who would put out the stars and deny the supernatural are powerless; they cannot get rid of Him.

God exists—eternally. He, too, has His rights. God will not suffer man to treat Him as an outcast with impunity, as One Who can be overlooked or got rid of; as One Who can be disposed of by an eloquent discourse, a vote, or a stroke of the pen.

But if we cannot find enough volunteers to counterbalance all these insults, what may we not expect?

In Claudel's *The Announcement Made to Mary* we find the subjoined passage: Anne Vercors, a farmer's wife of Combernon in the time of Joan of Arc, announces her intention of going to Jerusalem.

The mother: "What! you are going away? For good? And where are you going?"

Anne (*pointing vaguely toward the south*): "Yonder."

The mother: "To Château."

Anne: "Farther than Château."

The mother (*in a low voice*): "To Bourges, to see the other king?"

Anne: "I am going to the home of the King of Kings, to Jerusalem."

The mother: "Good heavens! Is not France good enough for you?"

Anne: "There is too much sorrow in France."

"Too much sorrow in France!" Yes, in very truth!

In the time of Abraham, two cities would have been spared if only ten just men had been found. And how greatly we need just men, how many more of them!

The Rev. Matheo Crawley, the well-known Peruvian missionary who has traveled all over France, has truly said: "For every social evil, I have found not simply one work of reparation, but a whole series of them."

If these good works are to flourish, we must have many, many souls of good will, souls eager to adopt a mode of life like that so aptly set forth in the subjoined passage:

"We must give up certain satisfactions and practice mortification, because others are suffering, and do these things with the greatest sympathy, because we feel drawn to share their sufferings. We must deprive ourselves likewise of certain pleasures, because others indulge in them to excess. In this case, we wish to ransom or compensate for their immoderation. So far as our position and powers allow, we try to maintain a certain level in the life of men."

Send us, O Lord, we beseech Thee, many of the just to make compensation for their brethren. May it please Thee to send us not merely faithful souls of the rank and file, but generous souls pledged to pay by their loyalty the ransom which Thy justice has asked for so long. Suffering alone will not suffice: we need suffering welcomed—*devota et pœnitens*—loving and penitent suffering. There are other urgent needs, but these are the most imperative.

But do yet more, dear Lord, raise up souls who, not content merely to accept suffering, seek and desire it as a means of restraining the power of evil. These are the souls who make reparation to the uttermost.

Cardinal Manning wrote: "We do not live in the age of martyrs (but, who knows?), but in an age when each must have the will of a martyr."

In a book written before the war, Daniel, the hero of the story, makes an excellent retort, which is likewise a rebuke, to a worldly young priest who was quoting with satisfaction the words of a bishop in China, who had witnessed many martyrdoms and speaking of them, said: "In my young days, I longed for martyrdom, but I do not want it now."

Daniel replied: "Let me tell you that if there are in France a thousand Christians, a hundred, or even twenty ready to suffer in their bodies the stigmata of the Passion, these alone are the true disciples of Christ and you may recognize them by their readiness to shed their blood joyfully. The earth on which we stand has drunk in their blood greedily, it was the blood of Sanctinus, of Blandina, and of Irenaeus. If France is to be born again, our blood too must be poured out."

Yes "our blood too must be poured out." Not perhaps on the battlefield or in the arena, but it must be shed drop by drop in our daily striving after holiness, and for the restoration of humanity in Christ. It must be given drop by drop by the daily sacrifices — often so trivial and yet meritorious — of an existence spent wholly for God.

The most faithful of these zealous souls give all to God, making the complete sacrifice of their self-love with all its manifold reservations, of their most cherished attachments, of their most legitimate pleasures and joys. They give all for the joy of seeing God at last known, loved, and served as He merits.

PART II

WHO SHOULD MAKE REPARATION

CHAPTER 4

Christians and Reparation

THE OBLIGATION OF PERFECTING or filling up the mission of Christ, and consequently His Passion, falls more especially upon those who are called by God to consecrate their lives to Him, but we cannot draw the conclusion that the ordinary Christian has no part in this noble work. On the contrary, each of the faithful both can and ought to assist and, in the measure of his generosity, enter the ranks of those consecrated to reparation.

The first reason for this, and one which should appeal even to tepid Christians, is *their own personal interest*. We all know the laws of divine justice. We know that as surely as God exists and cannot cease to exist, so surely crime will not ultimately triumph, but, sooner or later, sin will meet with its due punishment. God punishes sin sometimes upon this earth, but not often. He mercifully delays avenging sin in this world. After all, if man persists in his evildoing, God can satisfy His justice in eternity. But peoples and nations, as such, have but a terrestrial existence and, consequently, must pay the penalty of their evil deeds in this world. Their punishment here in some form or other is inevitable. This truth is strikingly exemplified in the history of the Old Covenant. Listen to the words of Jehovah addressed to the perverse Hebrews by the prophet Jeremias:

"The Lord said to me: Behold I will call together all the families of the North ... and they shall come, and shall set every one his throne in the entrance of the gates of Jerusalem and upon all the walls round about and upon all the cities of Juda. And I will pronounce My judgments against them, touching all their wickedness, who have forsaken Me ... and have adored the work of their own hands" (1:15–16).

Further on we read: "Behold I will bring upon you a nation from afar, ... a strong nation ... whose language thou shalt not know, nor understand what they say. Their quiver is as an open sepulchre: they are all valiant. And they shall eat up thy corn and thy bread: they shall devour thy sons and thy daughters: they shall eat up thy flocks and thy herds: they shall eat thy vineyards and thy figs. With the sword they shall destroy thy strong cities, wherein thou trustest" (5:15–17).

Note that God often makes use of a wicked nation — as we learn from the history of the Israelites — to give a salutary admonition or fulfill a glorious mission. Nor need we confine ourselves to past history; the present age provides us with striking parallels.

Undoubtedly, we cannot apply this law to any one particular case: we cannot assert as a positive fact that

Napoleon's exile and death in St. Helena was the expiation of his deeds at Savona and Fontainebleau, because the general law is one thing and its particular application another; and this general law is as follows: All crime must be avenged and God necessarily must triumph ultimately.

It is possible, looking at the Great War from one point of view, to assert—without committing ourselves to any paradox—that it was an act of mercy on God's part. On the other hand, it better fits in with the facts to look upon it as a punishment from God, as an act of divine justice. But men, blinded by pride, refuse to admit this explanation.

A soldier wrote as follows: "On all sides, agricultural implements, pierced with bullets, lie rusting on the ground. Tombs with their crosses are seen everywhere, in the middle of farmyards, in clumps of bushes, under trees. Tell me, is it not terrible to look upon *this vengeance of the Cross?* When shall we understand it?"

All who have gazed upon the innumerable cemeteries and thousands of tombs on the battlefields have felt this truth come home to them: "Men had banished the cross from their public monuments, their Courts of Justice, their schools and highways. Yet behold, the simple wooden cross is seen on all sides in the woods, along our highways, even in the midst of our gardens."

What were men so eagerly seeking formerly? What, alas! are they still too often seeking? Pleasure and enjoyment. Even in so many so-called Christian families, what license is tolerated! What contempt there is for the most stringent laws of God touching the sanctity of wedlock, the observance of the

Sabbath, and due respect for the good of our neighbors. All modern life is planned out with the view of escaping from suffering and from the inconvenience of complying with the binding precepts of God and of the Church.

Meanwhile, suffering bides its time, it prepares its revenge. Its hour came in August, 1914, when the war broke out. What anguish followed: there were separations, last farewells, constant anxieties. Weeks and months passed. Then news came: the loved one was wounded, a prisoner, or missing, or even worse than all these! Poor suffering creatures! What a capacity for pain there is in the heart of man!

None but those who were in the fighting line or on the vast fields of battle can imagine the amount of anguish, the multitude of sufferings that were crowded into certain hours, days, or even months of such an existence.

So much for the past, but what of the future? What remains of so many human joys, happy homes, and fair fortunes built up with such labor and trouble? Can we remain untouched by the sad vistas that open out and the inevitable sorrows that are foreshadowed? Can we do nothing to remedy this? Yes, we can do a great deal. During the war, there were three great armies — one to fight, one to nurse, and one to pray.

The army that fought paid its tribute to our country. It gave 1,300,000 lives. To their deaths, we owe our lives. The army of nurses showed boundless devotion. But perhaps the most powerful army, the one that most contributed to the victory, was the army of prayer and sacrifice, and to this belonged many of the soldiers of the two former.

St. Joan of Arc's words express a constant truth: "The hands that grasp the pike gain fewer battles than the hands lifted up in prayer." A grave writer has said: "The inexplicable victory of the Marne was perhaps won by the humble prayer of a little child. ... See that poor girl praying in some ruined sanctuary. She knows one truth, that God ever hears our prayers, since He has promised to answer the petitions of those who trust in Him. Listen, it is night and you hear the endless rumbling of an army on the march — infantry, cavalry, and impedimenta. All this noise comes from the prayer of an innocent girl whom God will surely obey."

These supernatural influences certainly played a great part in the history of the war, between 1914 and 1919. What will be their share in coming events? As great and as glorious as we choose to make it.

It is only too manifest that society is in the throes of a vast upheaval. Agitation prevails everywhere. Even more than in the past, the world has need of souls who are ready to ward off God's anger. Uneasiness and wild rumors predominate, convulsions rumble in the distance.

Would that we knew to what an extent we have it in our power to bring the divine action into the sphere of our human history! For this, it is not necessary to give up natural means; we have to use them, but we must teach Christians — even those who have little faith in supernatural helps — that these play their part in modifying the course of human events.

THE POWER OF REPARATION

He is powerful who acts upon the First Cause of all that is. Now the First Cause of *all*, in this world's history, cannot be *nothing*.

When St. Louis was setting forth on his crusade, a violent storm arose. The saintly king knelt for some time in prayer, then rising calmly, he assured his companions that the flotilla would make the voyage in safety. "How do you know that?" they asked. "Because," replied the king, "my monks of Clairvaux are praying and doing penance, so all will be well with us."

A few years ago, someone asked one of the bishops of China which was the best means of obtaining the conversion of that immense empire. "We must have some more Carmelites and some Trappists," replied the bishop.

Such means might seem totally inadequate for the required purpose, but we cannot go against the truth. What then is the truth? Well, think what ruins souls — sin. What saves nations? Holiness, and the two essential elements of holiness are prayer and penance.

From this follow two conclusions. First, we have to ask ourselves whether in our own lives in any degree, however small, we have ever contributed to bring about the state of things which we deplore so much. In certain Eastern countries, when a man has been murdered, the corpse is placed in some public place, and each citizen has to come forward in turn and, placing his hand upon the dead body, swear that he is innocent of the crime.

In presence of our country in such dire distress, we must not imitate Pilate and declare, as he did when judging our

Lord, that we are in no way to blame for these evils. Can we say how far the effect of our sins may have reached? Had there been more just men in Sodom and Gomorrah, these two cities would not have perished by fire.

Let us keep from sin. "What overturns nations? Sin." (*Quod evertit nationes? Peccatum.*) (Cf. Prv 14:34.) It is the sins of individuals which draw down misfortunes upon the people, far oftener than we imagine.

One single mortal sin *in itself* is sufficient to cause God to send some great calamity upon the earth. Very few understand this, and yet it must be said. For what is mortal sin? It consists in deliberately putting a creature in place of God, in ignoring Him, in desiring to do away with Him were such a thing possible. Now of itself the annihilation of all that is finite could never make adequate reparation for an insult offered to the infinite Being. These are the exact data of the problem, and whatever decisions men promulgate or accusations of cruelty they bring against God, the problem remains as before.

How many useful lessons we might learn even in our generation from the history of the Chosen People of God, if indeed the men of our age could still take any interest in the subject. Take the subjoined example: When the army of Israel marched against Jericho, one of the soldiers was guilty of a great fault. God had said all the booty was to be reserved for "the treasury of the Lord" (Jo 6:24) — i.e., for sacred purposes. Disobeying this command, Achan, an Israelite, took from the spoils "a scarlet garment exceeding good, two hundred sicles of silver, and a golden rule of fifty sicles ...

and hid them in the ground" (Jo 7:21). The army of Israel were defeated. Someone had disobeyed the Lord. The Lord of hosts left Israel to himself. The transgressor had to confess his sin and expiate it. "Then," said the Lord to the Israelites, "ye have won the day"—not, "ye shall win," but, "now ye have won the day." And, in fact, the Israelites then and there destroyed their foes.

Thank God, however, that under the New Law He does not often punish the masses for the crimes of individual persons. But, nevertheless, God can do so if He wills and in so doing He acts with perfect justice, since all the temporal punishments collectively cannot compensate for one mortal sin, seeing that there cannot be any approximation between the finite and the Infinite. Yet God, in His mercy, permits that sufferings inflicted by Him or voluntarily self-imposed by the Christian shall have the power of expiating faults. As our Lord said to St. Margaret Mary: "One just soul can obtain the pardon of a thousand sinners." In this way, without infringing on the rights of justice, God is able to exercise His mercy superabundantly. He frequently asks us to cooperate with Him to our utmost, so as to provide opportunities for Him to show His infinite mercy.

Our duty, then, is clearly marked out. We must not be scandalized, perhaps to the point of blasphemy, by occurrences that upset or distress us, as if we were amongst the pagans of today; we must not imitate the pharisaically faultless and self-righteous critics around us, who reject every explanation of historical events that accepts the principle of expiation. On the contrary, we must realize what sin really means and, in future, avoid it as the greatest evil whether for individuals or nations. It does not, of course, follow that given two nations, the most prosperous is necessarily the most holy, but the truth remains that, theoretically — if not always practically — a mortal sin can bring the greatest calamity upon the world and, if we have any care for the well-being of society, our first duty is to lead a good life and avoid those deeds which God, in His justice, cannot do otherwise than punish.

We should do well to meditate on what Newman writes on this question; in the light of what we have just said, there is no fear of our mistaking his meaning:

"Let us not conclude that God makes use of other punishments today (than of old) because we do not see His direct action. The principal difference between the punishments inflicted by God on the Israelites and on Christians is that the former were visible, the latter invisible — that is, we do not perceive these evils today as the chastisements of God, because God Himself or His chosen prophets no longer tell us this explicitly; but the effects of God's anger are no less real, and are even more terrible, seeing that they are proportioned to the greatness of the privileges which we have abused."

The task set before all Christians is not, however, purely negative. Each one, who desires to remedy or prevent sin, must place some counterpoise in the scale of God's justice. Alas! how many sins are committed in our land! For these, we must offer an ample measure of fidelity to prayer, acceptation of suffering, and progress in holiness. Hence every

Christian should make reparation, from a motive of self-interest. If he evades this obligation, the whole Christian body, all civilized society, an entire nation, may have to expiate his want of foresight or sinful indifference.

But there is another and a nobler motive; not that of interest but *love*.

Is it possible to see God so insulted without feeling impelled to make Him some compensation? Can we look on and see Christ our Lord, our Head, mocked at and treated as an outlaw without a feeling of indignation, of regret, or of deeper love for His cause? It is true that, from the days of His agony in Gethsemane and His Crucifixion, He is accustomed to have but few of His disciples with Him — but, even so, cannot we be of that number? Where is the faith, where are the noble sentiments that should animate the souls of baptized Catholics? Will none come forward to mitigate His sufferings? Will none try to comfort the Church in her grief? Are there only priests and religious who can realize what suffering costs and how much misery afflicts men?

"Look around you and tell me whether the world is governed by the Spirit of God Who created it, or by the spirit of Satan, the world's idol and destroyer? We must make reparation for all those who, though baptized by water and the Holy Ghost, have nevertheless sinned against Him. Yet we remain all the time indolent and inactive."[8]

The Holy Spirit is betrayed every hour of the day. Are there none willing to make reparation?

We see the Church of Christ continually attacked, now openly and shamelessly, now secretly and cunningly. Are we always going to remain inactive? During the battle of Eylau, Napoleon, seeing himself very closely surrounded by the enemy, called out to Murat: "Don't you see they are gaining ground? Will you let the fellows swallow us alive?"

If we can remain so indifferent, it is because we do not love our mother, the Church. The term *mother* is an empty sound, a mere mockery. Shall we suffer our mother to be insulted with impunity? Formerly, if anyone had grieved our human mother, should we not have striven to make amends to her by increased tenderness?

Msgr. d'Hulst writes: "We need in the world devout souls who love God and are desirous of making reparation and of doing it without stirring up the resentment or curiosity of their neighbors by their choice of means." Thanks be to God, there are some, more perhaps than we think.

It is related that a poor peasant woman was nursing her dying son. Presently, the young man, half-opening his eyes, exclaimed: "Mother, give me some water, I am dying of thirst." At this moment, the clock struck three. The Christian mother took a crucifix and, placing it in her son's hand in a voice broken by tears, said to him: "My dearest child, it is the hour when Jesus too was tormented by thirst and died for you upon the Cross. Won't you endure a little thirst to be like Him?" "Yes, Mother," replied the young man, and, putting the crucifix to his lips, he kissed it tenderly. Unconsciously these two, mother and son, were animated with the sentiments of St. Francis of Assisi when he exclaimed: "What, Thou, my Savior, art nailed to the Cross, and I am not nailed to it!" Their generosity puts these two among those "*good* Christians" of whom the saintly Curé of Ars once said: "Worldlings complain dolefully of having crosses; good Christians grieve when they have none" — amongst those who have understood what Fénelon calls "the great mystery of Christianity, that is, the crucifixion of man" in union with the Crucifixion of Christ.

True love ever begets imitation: this is the unequivocal mark of its genuineness. We subjoin a few examples.

Eugène Courtois, a member of the "Association Catholique de la Jeunesse Française," was killed in the September offensive of 1915. He was an honest workman, who had been converted by the example and influence of his dying brother. He practiced great austerities, rising very early in order to receive Holy Communion daily, sleeping upon a wooden cross which he placed each night in his bed even when he had a deep wound in his feet, nor would he have his wound attended to, because he desired to suffer. He devoted himself to tending the sick, whose ailments were most repulsive. He was never happy except when suffering, and frequently complained that his food was too good and that he had not enough privations.

Lucile X, when quite a child, happened to read the Life of Sœur Céline de la Présentation, who died in the Convent of the Ave Maria at Talence. Lucile resolved to imitate her by giving herself up to a life of reparation. She attended a mission at Maubeuge, which strengthened her resolution. In December, 1902, she made her First Communion, and, four years later, wrote thus in her spiritual notebook: "Jesus, I offer Thee the sacrifice of my life for my beloved country. . . . Make me suffer that I may expiate the crimes of France." In her piety and ardor, all is genuine and practical. She writes: "Self-renunciation consists in doing my duty, no matter what it costs me and without troubling in the least as to what I prefer. If I have a choice of two things, I will choose the most mortifying and will sacrifice my inclinations and do what others wish. I will never show any preference for a given thing nor use the words *I prefer*."

What wisdom this girl shows; how she understood true self-renunciation! She knew herself well when she said to God: "Send me suffering. Do not listen if I murmur when Thou answerest my prayer. O Jesus, do not cease to send me suffering: I give myself wholly to Thee." The divine Master ceased to send her trials when He called her home to Him on May 29, 1907.

The Curé of Ars used to say: "A Christian lives amidst crosses like a fish in the water." Yes, provided he seriously follows the teaching and example of his Master.

Madame Elizabeth of France in the prison of the Temple prayed thus: "My God, I accept all, I will what Thou willest, I sacrifice all to Thee, uniting it with the sacrifice of my Savior." Général de Sonis prayed: "Let me be crucified, Lord, but by Thee." In the terrible fire that broke out in Paris in the convent of the Sisters of St. Vincent de Paul, where a bazaar for their works was in progress, many fell victims to the flames. Among them was a young girl of twenty. In her half-burnt notebook, found on her dead body, were written these words: "O Jesus, I offer Thee my life as a ransom."

Little Bernadette Dupont asked God at her First Communion that she might become a religious and die a martyr. God did not answer the first petition, but accorded her the second. She died at the age of fifteen, after a painful illness of nearly three years.

Here is an example of a commanding officer. He was a Breton of noble birth. At one time he had almost decided to give up his military career, rather than sacrifice his faith. War broke out and he resolved to pursue it. Not content to remain in charge of home defense merely, he asked to go on active service. Passing by Domrémy, he visited the sanctuary of St. Joan of Arc, where he uttered this generous prayer: "I offer my life as a ransom for so many young men who are not guilty of the sins of their fathers." He felt that his offer was accepted by God. When placed with the third battalion of Zouaves, on starting out, he said to one of his companions: "The greatest honor of my life will be to suffer for my country." A few weeks after, he fell on the battlefield. The parish priest, his intimate friend, read the subjoined extracts from this brave soldier's letter:

"Does not our beloved country need voluntary victims, ready to offer themselves as holocausts for her ransom? If only God would accept me as a victim of expiation, as a ransom for our land, how gladly would I give my life for the sacred cause of reparation." "After having seriously considered the matter and prayed earnestly, in spite of the sentiment of my utter unworthiness, I have ventured to offer myself." "I do not know if, in spite of my faults, God will judge me worthy. But should He mean to hear my prayer, I thank Him in anticipation for all His kindness and indulgence."

Mirabilis Deus in sanctis suis (Ps 67:36). It is indeed admirable what God can effect with such a wretched thing as the heart of man. Let us admire it and, at the same time, try to understand it. Many know nothing of such heroic acts: those who perform them, generally speaking, do not realize their own heroism. There are different degrees of generosity and greatness in these deeds, ranging from the most glorious to the most humble (which are not always the least meritorious). Those who have heard of these voluntary victims know that there are more than we might imagine. Doubtless, specially privileged souls retain their high place and are consequently not numerous, but, as the examples just cited prove, God has chosen souls even in the world and among those who live an active life.

We have already given Fr. Matheo Crawley's testimony to the religious vitality in France. We will now give another quotation from his works:

"The generation of Christians, ready for daily sacrifices and even the greatest, that of their lives, is still in existence. We must not look upon it as a thing of the past. In the great centers and in the villages, I myself have come in contact with chosen souls, whose moral beauty was absolutely surprising. But they must be sought for. Like the hidden springs of water, they work secretly and silently. Their hidden virtues spread fertility all round. Everywhere, in every rank of society, among those in high position, among influential men as well as among the obscure and humble workers, God has His chosen souls.

"Whence do these priceless souls spring? They are the drops of blood of a noble race, the voice of the living traditions of the old Catholic stock, the moral wealth of an organism that is steeped in the purest and most virile Christianity. It is of this wheat that God has kneaded the reparatory victims (*nostras reparatrices*) of France."

It devolves upon us to cherish and guard these chosen grains of the purest wheat. If God has inspired us with the germ of generous desires, let us beware of the indifference that environs us. If we would be ready to suffer, we must love God. Is this so difficult?

On the 25th of Ventôse (the sixth month of the first Republican calendar), 1794, one of the judges of a revolutionary tribunal asked a saintly young girl—Marguerite de Pons: "What are your religious views?" To which she answered simply: "I love God with all my heart."

And who cannot make the same reply? Loving God with all our heart—that is equipment enough for starting on the work of reparation. That, too, is enough to keep us carrying it on successfully to the end.

CHAPTER 5

Religious and Reparation

"THERE ARE IN THE world some roads with never-to-be-forgotten names."⁹

One is the *Regina Viarum*, "the Queen of roads." Through Capua, Benevento, Brindisi, and the Ionian Sea, it put Rome in communication with Greece and linked together the two poles of the world. It was the highway of artists and poets.

Another is the *Via sacra*. It skirted the Palatine, crossed the Forum, and led up to the Capitol. It was the conquerors' road.

There is a third, the *Via dolorosa*. It starts from the citadel of Antonia—Pilate's residence, in Jerusalem—and runs by the houses of Annas and Caiaphas to the top of Calvary. This was the way followed by our Savior, and still trodden by all who wish to walk in the footsteps of the Crucified—the Sorrowful Way, or in the words of the *Imitation*, the Royal Way: "The Royal Road of the Cross."

Is not the essence of all religious vocation a call to unite with Jesus Christ in a special way? By sanctifying grace alone, God admits us to a marvelous intimacy, and we possess God in our souls. But if the title of *Spouse* can be applied strictly speaking to God, living in every one of the baptized, how much deeper is its signification when the soul is not merely engaged in the way of the commandments, but is chosen and marked out from all eternity for His special service, and is set apart by Him from the beginning, selected, attracted, and consecrated by Him.

Marriage consists in mutual engagements and the placing of the ring on the finger. Baptism can truly be called a marriage, since it consists of the union of God and the soul, but the term means far more when we refer it to religious, those souls of predilection with whom God is so intimately united in virtue of their vow of chastity.

It is part of the essential condition of the state of matrimony that husband and wife form but one. They share together all their projects, joys, perplexities, anxieties, sufferings, and trials. Their hearts are united and beat in unison.

If a religious is in earnest, if the soul is truly the spouse of Christ, this will be her prayer:

"Love for love, life for life, blood for blood, offering for offering: all is one between us. Thou canst no longer suffer, but Thou hast confided Thy mission to me, and, with my whole strength, I devote myself to this work. In order to make reparation to Thee and to assist Thee in saving the souls for whom Thou didst offer Thyself, I will suffer for those who live for pleasure; I will love for those who blaspheme; I will be humble for the proud; weep for sinners who laugh, and give Thee my whole soul for those who reject Thee.

"I hear Thy complaint; I hear Thee say: 'My love is unrecognized and persecuted. I seek a place of repose and I have chosen thy heart.' Like Sister Elizabeth of the Trinity, I will offer Thee a dwelling, a shelter in my soul, and there my love shall make Thee forget all the insults and outrages of sinners. I know that in my soul, in the inward 'temple' of Thy grace, Thou wouldst see an altar of sacrifice for Thy divine transformations set up. I will offer Thee the matter of the sacrifice, which by Thy divine presence and power, Thou wilt transform and divinize. Thou, in me, wilt offer Thyself to the Father and Thou wilt offer all without consulting me. Do not heed my repugnances nor resistance, suppress pitilessly whatever hinders Thy designs. Must I not 'be made perfect in one' (Jn 17:23) in order to work efficaciously for all to be united with Thee? If Thou art not wholly in me, how canst Thou be my All-in-All?

"Dear Master, long ago, by holy baptism, I received grace and Thou didst take possession of my soul. Henceforth, I possess Thee more intimately by my vows. Thou, by Thy power, wilt destroy in me all that is not Thyself. I yield up all my faculties to Thee. From now on, my path in the future is clearly traced out. My one aim shall be to repair the outrages committed against Thee by so many ungrateful sinners. In the rags of my spiritual poverty, I will strive to devote myself to Thy service, and though a poor substitute for Veronica, I have but a worn veil and an unworthy heart,

I will pass my life consoling Thee in Thy sadness, and binding up Thy wounds. I hold tightly the crucifix of my vows, of our reciprocal engagements. With Thy permission, I put my lips to Thy sacred wounds.

"I kiss the wounds in Thy hands as a reparation for those who do wrong; I kiss Thy forehead, pierced by the thorns, as an atonement for sinners who think not of Thee, or only remember Thee that they may outrage Thee. I kiss the wound of Thy Heart to atone for those who hate Thee and love evil.

"I would fain do more, for the truly devoted souls do more than say, 'Lord, Lord!' I long to prove my generosity by my acts, by imprinting upon my life, if not upon my body, the sacred stigmata of Thy Passion.

"Assuredly, what I offer Thee is but little and insignificant. Yet one thought consoles me. It needs so little flour to make an altar bread, only a few crushed grains. I will resemble that altar bread which will become the consecrated Host. To remind me of its littleness, I will adopt as motto: 'He must increase, and I must decrease' (Jn 3:30). To imitate its whiteness, my ideal shall be the purity of the angels, and in imitation of its immobility—for the Host is carried or placed as the priest wills—I will obey unquestioningly and instantly."

Such is the general outline of the spirit of sacrifice of a fervent religious. The consecrated life in itself presupposes the acceptance of a crucified life, but some chosen souls, desiring to go further than their rule obliges, aim at a life of continual and great suffering—the greatest possible. The desire of constant, radical, and unceasing immolation in all their actions is their ruling thought.

We have numerous examples of fervent Christians, who have given themselves to God without measure both in the world and in the cloister. They have responded to a very special call from God. But, leaving on one side these individual calls to reparation, and speaking of religious life as a whole, we assert that every religious vocation is necessarily a vocation for reparation. It is so of its very nature, whether considered in general or in detail.

All around we see more and more spiritual ruins, and laborers needed to restore them all. Many Christians murmur: "Yes, someone should attend to this, but why should I trouble?" Others, though few, humbly and yet resolutely say: "Yes, someone should attend to it. Why not I?" They start at once. They enter religion, inspired by the desire to make reparation.

Such souls are energetic, they go ahead, in spite of obstacles. Although friends strive to keep them back, they enter religion. *Magister adest et vocat te* (Jn 11:28). They have heard His call and they obey. What matters if they have to renounce the most sacred ties? With God's help, they are prepared to break them. St. Joan of Arc used to say: "If I had a hundred fathers and mothers, I would leave them." All aspirants to religious life reecho her words. "A hundred mothers!" How hard it is to leave *one* at such times! Yet in spite of all, they make the sacrifice. A firm determination does not prevent their suffering acutely.

"What are you taking with you into the convent?" "Nothing. Oh yes, a dozen handkerchiefs to weep to my heart's content." Just then one clings to the merest trifles, and yet goes on.

One says: "I must be off to the King." This is the last word of all who have heard the divine call: "Go, child of God, go forth," and to whom God gives the courage to respond.

The world knows nothing, sees nothing in such heroism. If it condescends to make any comment, it mutters: "Lunacy!"

"Lunacy!" Well, yes, we accept the impeachment. On one occasion, Abbé Gayraud, then deputy for Finistère, was defending the Religious Congregations in the French Chamber; the question of their expulsion was being discussed and the Abbé was praising religious and pointing out what greatness of soul it required to renounce the world, act as lightning-conductors for the anger of God, and lead a life of self-immolation in union with Jesus Christ. The orator spoke of the Brothers of St. John of God who devote themselves to the service of the insane, of the Little Sisters of the Poor, whose food consists of what is left from the table of the old people they tend, and who, with them, live on what they beg from door to door.

A deputy of the Left, extremely anti-Catholic, exclaimed impatiently: "They are all lunatics!"

"Yes, Monsieur Allemane," quickly retorted the Abbé, drawing himself up to his full height, the better to mark the moral littleness of his interlocutor. "Yes, they are lunatics. Their madness was diagnosed centuries ago by St. Paul as 'the folly' of the Cross"[10] (see 1 Cor 1:18).

After all, the logic of reason and of faith blended with the logic of the heart seems madness or folly to the world. Yes, folly there is, but not where the world thinks.

The folly of the Cross!

All who are victims of this madness have seen their crucified Savior passing by. He looked so sad and suffering. They heard His voice murmuring, "Follow Me." Instantly they felt impelled to give themselves to Him alone, to consecrate to Him their hearts, their youthful vigor, all their affections, all their love. Nor did this suffice; they longed to give themselves wholly and forever to do His will; they desired to suffer with Him and offered to follow Him whithersoever He should go, not only to Bethania, Thabor, and the Cenacle—that would be simple enough—but even to the Garden of Olives; to the Praetorium, where Pilate points Him out to the rabble, saying, *Ecce Homo* (Jn 19:5); even to the pillar of the scourging, where He is tortured and insulted till they reach the Cross on which He bleeds to death for the expiation of our sins.

Even to the Cross! They had often gazed at it, but never understood it. Custom prevents one from noticing. But now, for once, the cross appears quite different, be it the roughly hewn crucifix of the roadside or the elegant crucifix hanging over the bed. For the first time one realizes the true meaning of our Lord's words to Blessed Angela of Foligno: "My love for thee is not in play!" Not in play indeed! And one thinks: "There was a cross, a real cross of wood on a mountain, that showed it once. What a day was that! Besides all the crosses on which dead Christs hang, there was once a

Cross, on which the living Jesus hung bleeding, till He died on it for me, for all men." And thinking of Jerusalem and its blasphemy and ignorance—of the indifference and hatred of the world—one says: "How plain it is that if Jesus were to return to earth, He would be crucified again and even more quickly than before."

No sooner have we better understood the Passion of Christ and the world's hatred of Him than we see that life is altered. We repeat with Pascal: "Jesus Christ will be in an agony until the end of the world, and during this time we must not sleep."

Sleep forsooth! It ill befits us to sleep when the divine Master is hanging suffering upon His Cross. Alas! for how many His Passion is of no avail!

When David asked Urias, who had just come from the battlefield, why he had not gone home to sleep, he answered: "My Lord, Joab sleeps in a tent, and am I to lie down in a palace?" (Cf. 2 Kgs 11:11). After seeing Christ crucified, dare we shirk the cross?

To one, who applied for admission into a Carmelite convent, the superioress gave a vivid description of the austerity of the life behind the iron grill. "Is there a crucifix in each cell?" asked the future postulant. "Yes." "Very well, Mother, the rest does not matter; nothing will be too hard." The saints thought thus.

When St. Philip Neri was dying from sheer exhaustion, the doctor ordered him to take beef tea to recruit his strength. They brought it to him and he began to drink it. Presently he left off abruptly, and exclaimed: "Oh, my Jesus! what a difference between me and Thee! Thou wert nailed to the hard wood of the Cross, and I am on a comfortable bed. They gave Thee vinegar and gall to drink, and I have delicacies. Thou wert surrounded by enemies who insulted Thee, and I have kind friends around me, who strive to console me." The contrast made the saint weep so much that he could not take any more broth, although he was in such need of it.

Wherein lies the great secret of all attraction to a life of reparation, such as is led by religious? In the fact that Jesus was crucified, and they embrace the cross. He suffered, therefore they desire to suffer. Jesus was buffeted, and therefore they wish to be despised, ignored, forgotten, and even persecuted.

In one of our Lord's apparitions to St. Margaret Mary, He showed her two portraits of Himself. The one represented Him in His Passion, the other in glory. "Which wilt thou choose?" He asked her. Without hesitation, she stretched out her arms to the one representing Him in His sufferings. Yet, at the beginning of her religious life, this saint had endeavored to lead a holy life without any suffering. She had carefully sought for a saint who had not mortified himself and was finally convinced that such a one did not exist.

In the Life of the Comtesse d'Hoogworst, Emilie d'Oultremont, foundress of the Sisters of Mary Reparatrix, we read of her having a vision, similar to that seen by St. Margaret Mary. When in Rome in 1843, Jesus showed her His Sacred Heart. She says He came to her holding out two crowns, one of roses, the other of thorns. Without speaking or hearing one word, she instantly grasped the crown of thorns "with all the love of her heart" as she tells us, adding: "After that I always loved the crown of thorns."

Marie Deluil-Martiny, foundress of the "Filles du Cœur de Jésus," used to say: "If God gave me the choice, I should prefer the cross without consolation to consolation without the cross."

How can we explain this strange inclination, this unnatural attraction and inexplicable preference? We must attribute them to souls having discovered, more or less explicitly, that suffering alone can unite them to Him, Who is their All. As regards all else, the distance is too great, for on His side there is infinity, on theirs, nothingness; on His, unspeakable riches; on theirs, unutterable poverty. They could not contend with Him. Where, then, could they find something in common? In this: He has suffered; they can suffer. In all else, He is infinitely above them, for is He not God? But by their suffering they can walk with Him, the Sufferer. On this plane they can meet their God. The road by which He came to them is the road by which they can go to Him. The distance between God and the soul decreases. There is something similar in their lives, and God and the human soul, so different for all else, here have a certain resemblance. The "suffering" soul becomes for God "a helper like unto Himself," one less unworthy henceforth of His choice, His favors, and His embrace.

The biographer of St. Lydwine remarks that, within given limits, all Christ's devoted servants are called by Him to the work of expiation. Some, it is true, have a vocation that is not directly connected with it, since their special mission is to convert sinners, regenerate monasteries, preach the gospel to the poor, or they have some secret charge, known to God alone. Yet all these, notwithstanding, are asked to contribute their share of suffering to the common treasury of the Church; all have to give their Master the most genuine proof of their love—namely, that of self-sacrifice. Among these chosen souls there are some who are more particularly called to suffer as propitiation for sin. They are chosen to wear their Master's livery, and these victims include both men and women.

St. Francis Xavier, when dying on the coast of China, murmured continually: "Send me more suffering, Lord." St. John of the Cross had his motto: "To suffer and be despised." In the next chapter, we give several beautiful examples of priests who have lived a life of sacrifice. Many others could have been cited, among them those of Père de la Colombière, of Monsieur Olier, of Père Surin and Père Ginhac. Among the laity, Monsieur Dupont, "the holy man of Tours," holds a foremost place.

More generally, however, as Huysmans remarks, it is from among the weaker sex that God chooses His victims of expiation, a fact which this writer explains thus:

"God seems to have set women apart to pay the debt of sin. Men saints have a wider sphere of action and one that attracts attention. They travel all over the world, found or reform religious orders, convert the heathen, exercise their ministry in the pulpit by their eloquence. Woman has a more passive role to fulfill: she has not the sacerdotal character and may pass her life in silent suffering on a bed of sickness. The temperament of a woman is more affectionate and devoted, as well as less selfish than a man's. She is likewise more impressionable and susceptible of emotion. Our Lord Himself met with a readier welcome from women; they excel in little and refined attentions, little acts of thoughtful charity such indeed as a man, unless he is a St. Francis of Assisi, overlooks." Further, virgins vowed to celibacy have no outlet for mother-love so instinctive in woman; consequently they lavish all the wealth of their affections upon our Blessed Lord, giving Him the love of a spouse and a mother; for them, He is, as it were, both Child and Husband. The joys of Bethlehem appeal more to women than to men, whence it follows that they are more ready to respond to the divine call. Therefore, notwithstanding their changeableness and illusions, the divine Spouse finds His privileged victims chiefly among women.

St. Teresa used to say: "Let me suffer and die." St. Mary Magdalene de Pazzi amends her saying thus: "Let me suffer and not die."

Marcellina Pauper, a Sister of Charity who offered her life in expiation for the profanations of the Blessed Sacrament and the desecration of the Sacred Host, said: "My life is a delicious purgatory, in which the body suffers and the soul rejoices."

Veronica Giuliani, a Poor Clare of the eighteenth century, used to say: "Vive la croix toute seule et toute nue, vive la souffrance" ("Hail to the Cross only! Hail to the naked Cross! Hail to suffering!"). And Mère Marie du Bourg said: "If sufferings were for sale, I would rush to buy them." To these add the testimony of St. Lydwine, in the midst of her terrible pains of body and soul: "I am not to be pitied, for I am happy. If I could obtain my cure by reciting one *Ave Maria*, I would not say it."

Some readers may object: "These heroic souls lived long ago, there are none in our generation." The passage subjoined proves that such an objection is unfounded. It is taken from *A Religious Reparatrix*,[11] to which R. Bazin wrote the preface. This religious lived in our times. She writes: "I desire to suffer. I will suffer because Jesus has suffered for me and God asks for suffering as an expiation for the sins of the world. I desire suffering because it is the most powerful of all prayers, because it purifies and uplifts the soul. I wish to suffer because therein consists happiness and my soul is hungering for true happiness. *Non mori, sed pati.* I am ready to suffer for a hundred years, if needs be, in order to save souls and glorify God. I need, too, that strength of the soul, that key of heaven — namely, continual prayer. Prayer unites one to Jesus, and helps one to bear all things for His glory. Prayer is the sister of suffering; they both unite in giving themselves to God and saving the world. Jesus never put them asunder in His hidden life, His Passion, and when on the Cross."

Simone Denniel, another religious of the Sisters of Mary Reparatrix, used to say: "The roses for Him, the thorns for me. To be a victim with the Victim, a victim for the Victim, this must sum up my whole life."

In addition to these citations, many others from contemporary sources might have been given — for example, to name only a few, Xavérine de Maistre, Théodelinde Dubouché, Madeleine Ulrich, Thérèse Durnerin, La Mère Marie du Divin Cœur, and Caroline Clément. But besides these saintly women, whose lives have been made public, as a consolation and rebuke to the world, how many in silence and obscurity offer themselves as victims, gladly consenting to do their part toward the work of reparation, as victims known only to God.

Blessed be these living holocausts, known and unknown, for all the glory they give to the Lord of all, and for the protection with which they surround us, often without our knowledge. "Some people think that with cannons and ammunition our safety is secured. They do not know that side by side with the horrible progress of events on the battlefields, an inevitable mystical drama is being acted and the purest sacrifice being offered. It is the lamb, not the wolf, that takes away the sin of the world. When seated in the amphitheater of ancient Rome, the rhetoricians saw Christians devoured by wild beasts as an interlude; they looked upon the tragedy as an item of the entertainment and nothing more. How astounded they would have been had some prophet foretold that, from the blood of those Christians that soaked the arena, a new world would arise. If any man had ventured to assert that the catacombs were more to be feared than the Forum, what Roman magistrate would not have deemed him a mad man?"[12]

Thus it is in our days: the same law obtains that those who suffer and expiate in the catacombs are the first and most active laborers in the work of supernatural restoration.

CHAPTER 6

Priests and Reparation

GEORGE GOYAU, WHEN GIVING notice of the forthcoming publication of a book entitled *Priests' Letters to the Armies*, calls the Holy Mass "the greatest event in the history of humanity," and he adds:

"Daily, the priest brings the effective operation of our divine Redeemer to bear upon the destinies of the human family. By a supreme act, he interweaves the weft of our daily sins with the divine Ransom; above the chaos of both open and hidden faults, he raises the Victim. Our human history is continually being permeated with this divine sacrifice, a sacrifice both multiple and one. To many this sacred rite is a mere commonplace thing. Nevertheless, through the agency of the priest, they are present at the recurrence of the decisive moment when our guilty world, so justly disinherited, was suddenly put on the way to the plenitude of the supernatural life by the two mysteries of the Incarnation and the Redemption. God has chosen the priest to perpetuate these two mysteries, and no human catastrophe can draw him away from this duty, which from the day of his ordination is one, for eternity, with the very life of his soul."

We could not express more briefly the grandeur and the responsibility of the priesthood. What is the priest? One who carries Christ on through the ages. But Jesus Christ came upon earth to give, to His eternal Father, a Pontiff, a Priest who could adequately make reparation and expiation. The priest, therefore, who is charged to prolong, as it were, the role of Christ, ought to imitate Him by offering himself with Christ as an evidence of adoration and expiation. The priest who consecrates will therefore be a victim with Jesus. He does not understand his whole ministry if he confines it to the distribution of the Body of Christ, of the Word of God, of the forgiveness of Christ, and does not at the same time accept the role of victim like his Master, of Whom he takes the place and perpetuates the work.

All the years Jesus spent upon earth He was a Victim, but He was not satisfied with this, for He had determined to prolong His sacrifice by the agency of His priests. This He accomplished at the Last Supper, on the eve of His death; hence the Mass sets forth, without the shedding of blood, the immolation of Christ bleeding upon the Cross. Uplifted on Golgotha, Christ between heaven and earth will be a shield interposed between God's justice and man's sin.

Jesus' mediation will be accepted by God, because of His wounds and His Precious Blood poured forth. But Jesus is likewise the shield between heaven and earth, between God's justice and our sins in every Mass. Each "elevation" compensates for our manifold scandals; each uplifting of the Host atones for some decadence of ours, for our falls into sin, because the virtue of His blood and wounds lasts on. There are not two sacrifices, but this is the same as that of the Cross, though set forth differently. This is the formal teaching of the Council of Trent.[13]

How many of the faithful, who hear Mass, do not seem to have any knowledge of this adorable mystery! How many use prayers which have no reference whatever to the Mass, though perhaps appropriate for other occasions! How many know the term *Holy Sacrifice*, without any conception of the exact truth and stupendous reality with which it corresponds!

Paganism still lingers on here and there. An old rustic used to turn his back to the altar where the Mass was said on the Sunday and pray before an old crucifix—the souvenir of a mission—placed upon one of the pillars. To a Catholic who suggested his turning round since our Lord was on the altar, this peasant replied: "Your God, perhaps, is there; mine is here." Such ignorance is more widespread than is supposed.

But do those who know that the sacrifice of the Cross and that of the Mass are one and the same know likewise that they are strictly bound to offer themselves to God in union with the self-immolating Victim? This is obligatory, if they would assist at the Holy Sacrifice according to the spirit of the Church and the intentions of our Blessed Lord.

The necessity for the faithful of uniting their sacrifice with that of our Savior at Mass flows from several considerations, such as: the essential principle of sacrifice and its practice from the earliest ages; the most ancient tradition of the Catholic Church from its foundation; the common teaching of the Fathers of the Church; the Liturgy of the Mass; certain special ceremonies; and even the matter of the sacramental species, and so on.

As far back as we can trace the history of sacrifice as a religious rite, we find that the victim was offered as a substitution for the worshippers, who thereby expressed to God their sentiments of adoration and desire to offer Him some expiation. Now this substitution would merely be a pharisaical and material act if, by the ministry of the priest and in union with him, the faithful did not offer to God that which the immolation of the victim symbolizes—namely, the homage of their piety, and repentance.

When a Jew, under the Old Law, had a sacrifice offered for himself, he had to place his hand upon the victim, as a sign that he united himself with it. In the Mass, we are reminded of this rite, when the priest asks God to accept the oblation which is offered for himself and for all God's family as an act of propitiation. (*Hanc igitur oblationem servitutis nostræ, sed et cunctæ familiæ tuæ, quæsumus, Domine, ut placatus accipias.*—Canon of the Mass.) In the primitive Church, the Christians gave the bread and wine for the Mass, each contributing his share as a sign of his spiritual participation in the sacrifice. The Fathers point out that as many grains of wheat and many grapes are employed to produce the bread and wine used in celebrating the Mass, so the multitude of the faithful all united in one body must offer themselves to God. This glorious fundamental doctrine is always the same.

Christ is not complete without His Mystical Body, His oblation is only perfect when we unite ours with it.

Bossuet in his *Exposition of Catholic Doctrine*—a book written for Protestants—explains how Catholics hear Holy Mass. He says: "When we offer Jesus Christ to God, we learn to offer ourselves together with Him to the divine Majesty, in Him and by Him, as *living victims*." St. Augustine teaches the same doctrine: "When the Church offers the Body and Blood of Jesus Christ to God, she likewise offers and immolates herself. The true sacrifice of Christians consists in their forming one Body with Him."[14]

Unfortunately, so few of the faithful have any practical knowledge of this sublime truth, which ought to be known and practiced by all. If this be true of the Christian, how much more does it apply to the priest! "How gloriously the Church would stand forth if all her children (and we may add, all her priests) understood thus clearly the law of sacrifice. Along with Jesus, in appearance dead, all Christians spiritually sacrificed ought to form one *Victim of adoring reparation*. Grant, O Lord, that it may be thus with all of us; may it truly be thus. May we be immolated victims with our Eucharistic Lord."[15]

The priest who really understands what his Mass signifies and who would live up to it fully should do everything with his Host and nothing apart from Him. *Per Ipsum et cum Ipso et in Ipso*. All by Jesus as Victim, all with Jesus as Victim, all in Jesus as Victim. To live and not to live a crucified life should be to him unthinkable. Undoubtedly, the priest has his failings and defects, they are ever with him, but he will keep his ideal before his eyes notwithstanding and realize that since he offers the Holy Sacrifice, he must be a man of sacrifice.

When Msgr. d'Hulst was made subdeacon, his sister sent him a little picture, on the back of which was written: "Do not be a priest, without being a victim." This would be an excellent motto for all priests.

We have seen how a true, deep knowledge of the Holy Mass should logically lead every Christian, and still more every priest, to offer himself as a victim whenever he hears or celebrates Mass. In like manner, a true and deep knowledge of what *Holy Communion* really is ought to urge every Christian, and still more every priest, to make this offering of himself as a victim every time he receives Holy Communion.

We can look upon the Holy Eucharist from two points of view: as our incorporation with the life of Jesus Christ, and as our incorporation with His death. Both these aspects are equally essential, soundly doctrinal, and have the same claim upon Christian piety.

Yet, in practice, different people give these two points of view a very different reception. Most communicants, when receiving our Lord, look upon it as a means of union with the *life* of our Lord. But how few look upon the Holy Eucharist as a participation in our Lord's sacrifice and immolation—in a word, in His *death*—as St. Paul explains when speaking of this Sacrament (see 1 Cor 11).

As Bossuet says: "Because the death of Jesus is always represented in the Holy Eucharist, the imprint of His death should be stamped upon all the faithful, who ought to offer themselves as victims in union with the Son of God. Such is the power of the Cross, a power that is likewise ever living in the Holy Eucharist."[16]

St. Paul tells the Christians of Corinth that, at each Communion, they "show the death of the Lord till He come" (1 Cor 11:26), by which he means them to unite with His immolation, to incorporate themselves with Him in His death. The author of the *Imitation* develops the same truth: "As I willingly offered Myself to God for thy sins with My hands stretched out upon the Cross and My body naked, so that nothing remained in Me which was not turned into a sacrifice of divine propitiation, even so *must thou willingly offer thyself to Me daily* in the Mass as a pure and holy oblation, together with all thy powers and affections, as heartily as thou canst."[17]

In another passage, St. Paul asks: "Are not they who eat of the sacrifices, partakers of the altar?" (1 Cor 10:18). His meaning is clear if we remember the rites and symbolism of sacrifice in the earliest times. As the Corinthians, to whom he wrote, well knew, to eat of the victim was equivalent to placing oneself upon the altar and taking an active part as victim. To eat of the victim therefore identified the recipient with the victim. St. Paul reminds us that, under the New Law, this likewise holds good. The effect of our receiving the Sacred Host is to give us a participation with the Victim, to unite us intimately with Christ in His immolation, to put us *in communion* with Him—that is to say, to become one with the sacrifice and offer ourselves spiritually with it and consequently to crucify the "flesh with its vices and concupiscences"

(Gal 5:24). This involves giving over to our Blessed Lord our work, sufferings, and prayers, our whole selves, that they may be permeated with His spirit of sacrifice. We are told that, in the fourth century, after having received the Precious Blood in Holy Communion, it was the custom to touch the lips still moistened, and, with the finger, make the sign of the cross on the eyes, ears, and forehead. Let us, in virtue of our frequent contact with the Sacred Host, endeavor to purify and sanctify our affections and our thoughts, our heart, eyes, and all our members, all we have and are, and, to this end, strive to make the necessary sacrifices.

For as Grimal says: "If we desire to reap the fruits of the Holy Sacrifice by Communion without sacrificing ourselves, to be divinized by the sacrifice without immolating ourselves with it, we are simply aiming at living as parasites of the altar and seeking salvation without the cross."

Holy Communion, rightly understood, not only *divinizes*, but likewise *immolates:* it cannot do the one without doing the other. Further, rightly understood, it does not consist simply in a treasure received, but must be a treasure given by us; it is not just receiving a sacrifice, but giving a sacrifice to God. We cannot worthily receive the Victim of the altar, except on condition of offering ourselves as victims upon the altar in a spirit of adoration and expiation.

On this subject, Msgr. Batiffol says: "Christian piety will always be more attracted by the Johannine presentment of Holy Communion as a participation in the divine life of our Blessed Lord, than in the Pauline presentment of it as a participation in His sacrifice, which will always have a darker aspect."

Will this verdict be revoked one day? May we not hope that when our priests have studied more deeply St. Paul's doctrine on communion with the sacrifice of Jesus, they will then be better prepared to teach the faithful to offer themselves as victims, whenever they are united with Jesus, the Victim? There are not enough souls willing to make reparation. Is this by chance because there are not enough priests who have a deep insight into the mystery of reparation? How can Christians know it, if those charged to distribute the Word of God are ignorant of this doctrine, or if, though conversant theoretically with the grand teaching of St. Paul on Holy Communion, as a participation in the sacrifice of Christ, they neither live up to it, nor exert themselves with all their energy to spread the knowledge of this truth?

Grimal, in his *The Priesthood and the Sacrifice of Jesus Christ* writes: "The great lesson of the Sacred Host is the spirit of sacrifice. The Eucharist reenacts the drama of the Cross.... The immediate and necessary effect of Holy Communion is to unite us to Jesus as Victim—that is, to Jesus immolated and immolating.

"Hence, the perfect communicant is he who sees Jesus Crucified and enters into His state of being a Host. Although the Christian may be in a state of grace and full of pious sentiments, yet if he does not receive our Lord in this spirit of sacrifice, he does not experience the grace of this Sacrament in all its plenitude. He does not understand the meaning of the Host (Victim); it may be owing to his having been taught to esteem rather those virtues connected with the Holy Eucharist, which are of minor importance compared with the one essential thing. If the faithful fail to see the cross ever present and vital on our altars, it may be because they have not been shown it plainly enough."

This same writer continues: "In our sermons on the Eucharist, our great object must be to explain that the Mass is the living memorial of the death of our Lord, so as to inspire our hearers with *that spirit of immolation, which will make them victims with Jesus in their daily lives*. ... Let us not fear the reproach of insisting too strongly on the harrowing side of Christianity, on the Passion and on the Christian's offering his life and death as a sacrifice of immolation. Could we do otherwise? Could we modify or veil the chief dogma of the Faith and of our salvation? Let us preach this doctrine in all its plenitude—that the Cross is perpetuated in the Eucharist and ends in heaven; that the Cross is the portion of the believer and of the communicant, who sacrifices himself by it, that he may live eternally; that the Cross, in all ages and more especially in our times, has a special attraction for privileged souls, for the purest and the noblest, for the lovers of suffering, for the sake of carrying on and continuing the Passion of Jesus. Who can describe the beauty and the fecundity of the Cross when it rules all the faithful? Who can describe the beauty and fecundity of these chosen souls, who draw their spirit of sacrifice from the Sacred Host and, immolated with Jesus, are the fragrance and the salvation of our poor earth?

"Grant us, O Lord, to be numbered with these souls. Grant that we may help to increase their number by our teaching and direction."

At the present day, there is a great increase in devotion to the Blessed Sacrament which Rome favors in every way, encouraging frequent and daily Communion. Let us therefore endeavor to induce all who approach the altar so often to communicate in the sacrificial spirit, as "hosts" (victims). It is not enough to practice certain mortifications, we must lead lives of mortification, embracing eagerly those numerous occasions of conquering self which occur all day long. We can do even more. In the tabernacles of our altars, Jesus, although alive, is in appearance dead. He permits the priest to handle and distribute Him at will. A holy soul writes as follows: "I think that the greatest act of which the soul is capable is to abandon herself entirely to God together with all she can do, suffer, and merit; to allow God to dispose of her as He wills, and to let this donation be known only to Him and to her. This oblation is the soul's highest act, because it gives the greatest glory to Jesus as Victim, because it strips the soul of all she has and is. By this act of homage to Jesus as Victim, the soul enriches Jesus' voluntary poverty by the gift of all the creature can possess and give. ... This donation of our whole being to God ought to be the habitual state of those who unite with Him frequently in the Sacrament of His love, since this self-abandonment is a strict condition as well as the necessary effect of eucharistic union with Jesus. ... The bitterest sorrow comes to the Sacred Heart from those who are ... selfish and forget that they are called to complete its *expiation and intercession* for all men, and hence no longer belong to themselves."

Certainly, many of these would profit more if, instead of communicating to satisfy themselves, they did so to please Him — that is, if losing sight of their interests they sought before all His interests. This is the eucharistic ideal of all communicants who are eager to expiate.

At the outset, a compassionate love is that which predominates in those consecrated to reparation. They deplore the contempt, indifference, and insults offered to God, the ignorance and negligence of men, the persecutions, crimes of the wicked, faults of good people, even of the best, of those even whom our Lord calls "His own," for, among His specially chosen, there are some unhappy falls. For all these wrongs, fervent souls desire to compensate our Lord. Knowing their Master to be so often alone, they visit Him. Since our churches are so empty when daily Mass is said, they will hear as many Masses as possible. In these empty churches, so few approach the altar, therefore they receive the living Bread daily; thus reparation leads to the Eucharist.

Then, changing the roles, the Eucharist leads fervent souls to a spirit of reparation. The Eucharist is no longer regarded from the outward point of view as of little value from being everywhere in the tabernacle, but the Eucharist is considered and understood as what it really is — namely, as the means of giving Jesus, who is Life eternal, hidden as a Victim, to all men. The bread and wine are but dead appearances: the faithful communicant is a living appearance of our Lord. What this means in the way of immolation we have pointed out. The altar of sacrifice will always be the great school of sacrifice.

It devolves upon priests to acquire and impart to the best of their power a clear, deep knowledge of the Sacrament, *par excellence,* of reciprocal love.

Now, unless a priest has lost sight of the aspirations of his youth and the obligations of his ordination, he must admit that with his desire for the priesthood were mingled ardent dreams of self-sacrifice, and that, on the day of his ordination, when he vowed fidelity to his high calling and binding engagements, he likewise had the set purpose of giving himself up wholly to a life of immolation.

The aspirations of his youth! What ardent desires are stirred up in a boy by reading the lives of St. Francis Xavier, Père Damien, the apostle of the lepers, of the Curé of Ars or of some missionary of Alaska or of Africa! *Non potero quod isti et istæ?*[18] "Can I not imitate what these have done for Christ?"

When they were quite little, their mother trained them to look steadfastly at the crucifix. There are some truths well learnt from a saintly mother. The hearts of children gather that something quite unusual happened on the Cross, something that bound them now and in the future. Jesus there offered Himself for them; they then must offer themselves to Him. What else was to be expected? In one way or another they imitate the little boy who had heard about the Passion of our Lord; he put his back to the wall and, stretching out his little arms in the form of a cross, he asked his nurse to drive nails through his hands and feet. How could he be "so well" when Jesus was "so ill"?

A child has a true and deep insight into things, especially if he has been brought up at home in the doctrine of self-sacrifice. Some parents are quite careless about this item, but there are others for whom this "item" holds the first place in the education of their children. They teach them to punish themselves, to deprive themselves of what they like. They not only teach them how Jesus suffered for them long ago, but also how the Church is suffering now; they instill into them the truth—though not perhaps explicitly—that God expects something from them when they grow up. We will cite a few examples of such teaching: When the enemies of religion were making the "Inventory" at a certain church, a Christian father went to protest against this injustice. He took his little boy with him, and lifted him up, that the child might see how Catholics were defending God's rights.

During the French Revolution, Msgr. de Quélen being then a child, his mother took him to visit the Carmelite priests in prison, that he might see how badly they were treated.

Madame Varin felt certain that one of her sons, Joseph, was called to the priesthood, but the boy would not hear of it. Frequently she would call the younger children around her, saying: "Let us say a Hail Mary for Joseph, who is not following his vocation." When dying on the scaffold, she offered her life that he might no longer resist the divine call. God heard her prayer, and as a priest Joseph Varin was called to do great things for God.

Priests and Reparation

In addition to his early aspirations, the priest has the call of his ordination; he cannot forget that in obeying it, he fully purposed to lead a life of self-immolation. When on that memorable day — so far off perhaps, and yet always so near — the young aspirant, clothed in his white alb, lay prostrate before the altar, his heart throbbing with emotion, and offered himself to God, did he not intend that, henceforth, his occupation, his one ambition, should be to lead a life of immolation, in union with his crucified Master? The bishop said, "Receive power to offer the Holy Sacrifice"; and then, "Thou handlest the paten and the chalice, the instruments of the sacrifice. Remember they are the instrument of thy sacrifice as well. *Imitamini quod tractatis.* It will be thy charge to handle the Sacred Host. Remember every morning when thou holdest the Host in thy fingers to live as a host thyself. *Quatenus mortis dominicæ mysterium celebrantes, mortificare membra vestra a vitiis et concupiscentiis procuretis.* Christ is dead; thou must lead a life of mortification — a victim along with thy Victim. Thus only canst thou be a true priest: see thou to this. Be it thy chief care to harmonize and synchronize thy life with that of Christ, thy oblation and immolation with His."

Monsieur Olier writes: "I loved to peep into the churches through the half-open doors, and, looking at the burning lamps, used to say to myself: 'Happy lights, that are entirely consumed for the glory of God and that ever burn in His honor.'" It is the office of the priest to consume his life thus, since he must be, like our Lord, he who sacrifices and that which is sacrificed. If all Christians are exhorted to offer their bodies "as living sacrifices" (Rom 12:1), how much more is the word meant for priests—priests who say daily: "This is My Body."

True priests give us grand examples of their faithful imitation of Christ as Victim, showing clearly that they looked upon it as the essence of their priesthood.

Abbé Perreyve asked three gifts of God on the day of his ordination: that he might never commit a mortal sin; that he might always remain a humble priest; that he might shed his blood for Jesus Christ. As a symbolic sign of this last request, he celebrated his first Mass vested in red—the color of blood.

Some time before this generous soul went home to his God, he wrote a meditation on the death of a priest in which he says: "Priests ought to look upon death as one of the functions of their priesthood. It is their last Mass." Following the example of Jesus, the chief use they must make of their bodies—"an essentially priestly use"—is to sacrifice them. "They must commence this death by the practice of chastity, continue it by mortification, and end it by their actual death, their last oblation and sacrifice. Like Thee, O Lord, they should prepare for death long beforehand."

A young cleric, in minor orders, of the Seminary of Nevers, who died on April 6, 1907, left the subjoined spiritual will: "I commend my soul to God, in union with our Lord dying on the Cross. I desire like Him, with Him, and in Him, to die a victim. This should be the character of my whole life by my vocation and by duty; may it be that of my last moments. ... I desire to live in God, detached from myself, so that He may reign absolutely in my soul. Joyfully I offer my divine Master the salutary sufferings of my last agony and the sacrifice of my life in *reparation* for the care I have so often taken to avoid suffering and mortification. I offer my life likewise for the Church, for France, for my family."

During the war, many, thinking that God would ask of them the supreme sacrifice, offered themselves wholly to God for life and death.

Père Gilbert de Gironde wrote: "How glorious it would be to die young as a priest and like a soldier in a battle, when marching to an attack, while exercising my priestly ministry, perhaps in the act of giving absolution! How grand to shed my blood for the Church, for France, for my friends, for those whose ideal is the same as mine, and also for others, that they may experience the joy of believing!"

Another priest, Abbé Liégeard, from the Grand Séminaire de Lyon and a corporal of the twenty-eighth battalion of Alpine "Chasseurs," offered his life "that the misunderstanding between the people of France and their priests might cease."

Fr. Frederic Bouvier, S. J., one of the most learned of the historians of religion, said: "I give my life for my companions in arms of the eighty-sixth battalion, that the many upright, good men, whose one defect is living without God and neglecting their faith, may turn to Him."

A seminarist, Abbé Chevolleau, corporal of the 90th Infanterie, wrote this in one of his letters: "Pray that I may abandon myself wholly to God. What matters life, the prospect of offering the Holy Sacrifice, of saving souls later on, if God asks me to offer myself as a ransom today?"

THE POWER OF REPARATION

This reminds me of two military chaplains—Père Gabriel Raymond and Abbé de Chabrol—two dear friends, whom I must mention.

The former, a friend of old standing, succeeded me in my little hut in the front line at Artois; the latter I replaced at Tracy-le-val in August, 1916. From the way in which both chiefs and soldiers spoke of their devotedness, it was certain that they could not escape death—they were too daring. We shall never know what acts of heroism these two priests performed: they were so brave, so calm, so unconscious of their merits. Père Raymond was crushed under the roof of a shelter.

A report of an attack thus attests Abbé de Chabrol's courage: "The waves of assailants gave way one after another before God's representative, the chaplain of the division, Abbé de Chabrol, as he stood bravely under fire with his hand raised, making the sign of our redemption and of victory." He was shot down in a fierce engagement, after having offered his life for the redemption of the world and for victory, as Père Raymond and so many others have done.

One more example in conclusion: Père Lenoir, a military chaplain, died on the field of honor on May 9, 1917. He fell a victim to his bravery in succoring the wounded. The Lieutenant-Colonel read to the regiment to which this zealous priest had devoted himself for two and a half years, and for which he had given his life, the following few lines, which were found on his body:

In Case of Death.
I bid farewell to my beloved children of the 4th Colonial Regiment.

From the depth of my soul of priest and friend, I implore them to make sure of their eternal salvation by their fidelity to our Lord Jesus Christ and to His law, by seeking the pardon of their faults, and by uniting themselves to Him in Holy Communion as often as they can.

I bid them all meet me in heaven. Also for this intention, I joyfully make the sacrifice of my life to our divine Master, Jesus Christ, for them.

Blessed be God! Long live France! Long live the 4th Colonial Regiment!

P. Lenoir.

Abbé Buathier, in his book *The Sacrifice*, has this exquisite passage: "Some unknown soul leaves this earth a hundred yards off; no one knows or cares. A few neighbors just make the commonplace remark, 'She is dead.' That is all: there is nothing else for the eyes of the majority.

"But this humble hidden soul had united herself with the Victim of Calvary, she realized the magnitude of the act she was performing. She knew that not only was she satisfying for her own debt of sin, but likewise paying for others—that she was increasing her own merits and bequeathing this treasure to the Church. She knew that by her death she could give life to many and offer them to Jesus: she knew, willed, and longed for all this. Her oblation ascended to heaven, and, in the midst of her agony, her sacrifice was consummated; her soul was inundated with that joy which is a foretaste of peace and the beginning of eternal glory.

"For her, as for our crucified Savior, death had only been the supreme act of love. Men see nothing in it, but angels look on in admiration, and God awards His crown."

Was there not something of this in the deaths we have described?

Some years ago it was said: "The Church of France needs saints." The Church of France has had them, she still has them. The examples given prove it, and many more might have been given. Let us hope that, some day, we shall know them all, together with the particulars of their lives. Nevertheless, we must bear in mind that the war, which revealed so much holiness and heroism, created neither the one nor the other.

It was no sudden impulse, no mere chance, which urged these brave Christians to offer their lives as acts of reparation, in union with their divine Master. It was, in each case, the result of a long preparation, a volition. It was no improvisation, but a calculated result. It was the daily self-denial in the drab environment of daily life, the practicing of mortification, chastity, and zeal, which prepared the soul to offer herself so spontaneously, generously, and totally a victim, and to accept the crucial act of the closing of life.

These brave Christians, let us remember, died, as we have seen, only because they made "a long preparation for death."

PART III

HOW REPARATION SHOULD BE MADE

Preliminary Note

Although all Christians should make reparation, they should not all do it in the same way.

The mother of a family might make reparation, but certainly not in the same manner as a Carmelite.

There are three factors which play their part in deciding to what extent each Christian, individually, can volunteer to walk on the Royal Road of making reparation. These three factors are:

1. *The duties of our state of life.*
2. *The leadings of grace.*
3. *The sanction of authority.*

Bearing these in mind, we must likewise remember that there are two degrees of self-oblation to a life of reparation. Taking for granted the acceptance of suffering from the motive of love as the essential principle of reparation, Christians will be divided in proportion to the measure in which they devote their lives to the Cross.

CHAPTER 7

How We Can Make Reparation by Leading a Simple Christian Life

PEOPLE ARE TOO PROMPT to think that, in order to consecrate themselves to a life of reparation, they must necessarily live in a cloister, practicing silence and the most severe austerities of Christian penance. This is a mistake.

Reparation is not so much the observance of certain fixed *practices* as a *spirit* which adapts itself readily to any mode of life, provided it be truly Christian.

"The *spirit* of reparation." Hence, before all, it is necessary to bring home to ourselves and to weigh the fact that our Lord was crucified—crucified for us—and that we must help Him; to discover those around us—and how many there are!—who are being lost. This seems a small matter, but how many Christians know nothing about it! If we live guided by these two great thoughts, we possess the spirit of reparation.

THE POWER OF REPARATION

As Chanoine Leroux of Brittany writes: "The life of reparation is not in itself a particular form of the Christian life," yet it is not the common life found among all Christians. Why not? Because, on the one hand, we should try to realize what the Christian ideal really means, and this is rarely done. On the other hand, "all those who are drawn to seek holiness do not all look at it from this particular point of view."[19]

But no sooner do we possess this spirit of reparation than we see all that it demands of us. We realize that, above all, we must be true to our baptismal vows, and keep the commandments of God and of the Church, not with a fidelity such as the generality of Christians offer God, but with an observance more integral and precise, without bargaining with God or seeking pretexts for escaping from our obligations. To serve God thus loyally in our private, social, and domestic life already opens out wide vistas.

An American author has written a story called *In His Footsteps*. The story commences with a minister who is preaching his Sunday sermon on 1 Peter 2:21: "Unto this are you called, because Christ also suffered for us, leaving you an example, that you should follow His steps." He delivered his sermon, to which his audience listened with their customary respect, but suddenly an old beggar interrupted him by calling out: "What! are you not ashamed? You dare to sing,

> Jesus, I my cross have taken
> And left all to follow Thee,

How We Can Make Reparation by Leading a Simple Christian Life

and yet live as you do!" Having said this, the beggar fell down dead. There was great consternation among the audience, greater still in the soul of the pastor. On the following Sunday, he proposed to his flock that they should form an association. Each member was to engage seriously for one year to ask himself, before each action: "What would Jesus Christ do in these circumstances were He in my place?"

A fair number joined the association — merchants, journalists, politicians, and so on. No sooner have they pledged their word than they find that they must change their lives. A certain Mr. Norman, editor of the local newspaper, is one of the members. They bring him an article on the races—three and a half columns of print. He asks himself: "If Christ were the editor of this journal, would He allow this article to stand as it is?" He decides in the negative, and the article is destroyed. The same fate overtakes other articles, political, commercial, and likewise some advertisements, with the result that the journal ceases to exist.

We see the gist of this story and its exaggerations, but we can profitably retain something of the underlying principle. How perfect would be our Christian life if, like these imaginary personages of this American story, we were to ask ourselves before each action: Were Jesus in my place and in these circumstances, how would He have acted? It is easy to see what a sudden change this would effect in the conduct of individuals, in relations between nations, in the life of families and of society.

A writer dealing with the question of the fall in the birth rate — a vital matter in these days, and one which convicts many Catholics of having failed in their duty—gives this title to his book: *France Repeopled by Practical Catholics.* The title suggests a scheme while passing a sentence of condemnation.

In no sphere can reparation be made except by the assistance of true Christians. These must not fail to accomplish their task; they must be Christians to the backbone, fearless and "shameless," as Louis Veuillot explains.

Generous souls will always find numerous occasions of practicing their faith to the point of sacrifice. In an earlier chapter, we have blamed the tendency, so common with many, to seek the least discomfort possible in their religion. Cardinal Manning writes: "We live in easy times. Who fasts nowadays? Undoubtedly the Church is very indulgent. Nevertheless, at the present time, the Jews keep strict fasts annually, taking no food from sunrise to sunset, a sharp reproof to us who are disciples of Jesus Crucified."

What terrible sufferings some of our soldiers had to endure during the recent war! For example, the Marine Fusiliers, who, during the famous campaign of Dixmude, had to stand in water for twenty-six days, with no other food than some tins of jam. Doubtless the cause for which they suffered was worth the pain, but is the cause of Christ less noble, though for this we dole out our sacrifices? Look around! See what men endure for the world, for fashion. And we ourselves, what are we doing for souls, for Jesus Christ?

The crucifixes that please us must be artistic, not too harrowing, made of ivory, mounted on velvet. But remember, these are not the true ones. The real crucifix is rough and it hurts.

When Heraclius recovered the Cross from the Persians of Chosroes, who had kept possession of it for fourteen years, desirous of carrying it to the summit of Calvary himself, he put on his most beautiful robes, his diamonds, and his imperial crown. But the bishop of Jerusalem objected, saying: "No. This cannot be. Do you not see the contrast between your luxurious robes and the bare Cross?" Then the Emperor exchanged his gold and pearls for a hair shirt. The Cross of our Savior is one that crucifies.

Hence, what a contradiction it is for Christians professing to follow Jesus Christ, to take such pains to avoid the most ordinary penances imposed by the Church! Cardinal Manning asks them with a touch of humor: "Allow me to ask you whether you believe your neighbor when he tells you that he cannot fast, nor keep the prescribed abstinence, that it affects his health, and so on.?" And he adds: "I have no scruple in arousing the conscience of some of you, for I am convinced that we are living in an effeminate age, which tends to do away with the gentle severity of the laws of the Church."

Whence it is manifest that we need not seek further. Simply by keeping these commandments strictly, or always in spirit, we have numerous opportunities of offering God very meritorious sufferings and privations, as acts of reparation.

Secondly, not only must we accept the mortifications imposed by the Church, but likewise those imposed by circumstances, such as reverses of fortune, bad health, bereavements, misfortunes, trials of all kinds. They abound; life is full of them, and is represented by a lyre with seven strings, of which one symbolizes joy and six suffering.

THE POWER OF REPARATION

Bossuet compares our moments of real happiness to brass-headed nails that stud a door. They appear numerous afar off. Draw them out and you have scarcely a handful. Like the stepping stones of a ford, our joys are unstable and far apart.

"Who art thou?" Beatrice asks one who is watching Dante's boat as it glides by. "My name? Do you not see that I am a weeper?"

"A weeper." Does not this define every man in this world, at least at certain moments? Hence, how sad it is to see how few are able to benefit by the tears they shed! Every one of us, with the total of sufferings which his life involves, has means of acquiring immense merits. Most men make no use of them; they do not trouble about the matter. Instead of utilizing their crosses for heaven and souls, they waste them, reaping no benefit from them, and only find in them occasions of sin, because of their rebellious feelings.

What should we say of a man possessed of a fortune all in gold if, instead of putting it into the bank as an offering toward the restoration of national historic monuments, he were to stand on a bridge and throw the coins, one by one, into the river?

Is not our first impulse, when suffering overtakes us, to complain against God? Our Lord once said to St. Gertrude: "I wish that My friends would not think Me so cruel. They ought to do Me the honor of thinking that it is for their good, their greatest good, that I sometimes force them to serve Me by doing hard tasks, and at their own expense. I wish that, instead of being exasperated by these trials, they would see in them the instruments of My paternal bounty."

The elite of Christians grasp this truth. We give a few examples.

A young religious was attacked by a terrible illness, which carried him off very suddenly. The parents knelt by his corpse. Then followed this dialogue: "We will say the *Te Deum*; do you agree?" "Oh, yes, with all my heart."

Ampère had just married and his future appeared bright. Suddenly, his wife was seized with a serious illness. In the depths of his sorrow he had the courage to write this passage: "O my God, I thank Thee. I feel Thou willest that I should live for Thee, that my life should be wholly consecrated to Thee. Wilt Thou take from me all my happiness here below? Even so, Lord, Thou art the Master; I have deserved this chastisement. Perhaps Thou wilt yet yield to the pleading of Thy mercy." What a power there is in strong, deep faith!

A mother heard that her son had been terribly mutilated by a shell. He was a man of great courage, and she wrote this letter about him to a friend: "He suffers a veritable passion in union with our dear Lord. It is wonderful to see this young fellow, crucified, stretched out on his cross of agony, and yet so happy, while suffering a martyrdom every moment. I thank God for linking him with the redeeming sufferings of the Cross. In our grief, we do not understand the mysteries of mercy which these trials conceal, but I believe that in heaven we shall know the price of these cruel immolations and that our dear invalids are very powerful in God's sight."

This young man intended to become a priest, so his mother adds: "What matters *how* we give, so long as our Lord takes what He wills, and gets all the glory He desires from His poor creature? ... If my son cannot be a priest, he can be a victim and share the role of Christ; who would complain at being treated like the Son of God?"

Shortly after this man's legs had been amputated, one of his brothers was killed. Still the brave mother shows nothing but brave resignation; she writes: "Only one more victim after so many others. God gave him to us that we might lead him to heaven. He has reached his goal. It seems so simple, but for us whose faith is so weak, how hard it is!"

How many mothers, sisters, and wives, bereaved by the war, have resolved henceforth to live as mourners. It might have been otherwise had they been courageous enough to transform the sacrifice imposed by God into a sacrifice willingly accepted, if they had said to their heavenly Father: "Lord, I thank Thee for permitting me thus to share Thy Cross. Father, Thou didst ask for *my boy's* blood, Thou askest for *my* tears; I give Thee all. I should never have had the courage to ask Thee to take my loved one, but since Thou hast taken him, I will be brave enough to say that Thou hast done well.... I understand and ratify Thy act. If I cannot say *Alleluia*, at least I will whisper *Amen*. So, it is well."

Another mother, speaking of her son who had fallen on the battlefield with many others in a glorious and costly campaign, wrote in confidence to a friend: "You know that I gave him up to God at the commencement and now I not only *accept* the sacrifice, but *will* to offer it to God. I place it

How We Can Make Reparation by Leading a Simple Christian Life

in His hands." The writer underlined these two words, *accept* and *will*.

"My poor heart cannot reconcile itself to its solitude, and it desires ardently to give itself more fully, to offer itself wholly to God." Thus wrote one of the many brave women widowed by the war. O blessed yearning! May our Lord give it to many souls. She goes on to say that her love, "too human perhaps, will now become more supernatural." This is just what God wants, probably it was why He permitted the trial. Finally, she prays "for great courage in offering herself more and more to God."

The excellent nuns who have charge of the Sanatorium of Villepinte have founded for their patients a "Guild of Thanksgiving." One of these young people hesitated about joining, saying: "I fear I shall not be able to say 'Thank you' to God when I suffer."

The practice of offering ourselves to God as a victim of love and reparation is an admirable means of overcoming this fear. It would be an excellent practice for so many suffering souls, who are paralyzed by the shock of recent events.

St. Jane de Chantal used to say: "The great wealth of the soul is to suffer much lovingly." Real Christians know the truth of this.

Père Ramière writes: "The soul can unite itself to God by prayer, and likewise by work, but that which most intimately unites the soul to God is suffering accepted for God, offered to God, and loved for God. Such suffering is the best of all prayers, the most fruitful of all toil." Père de Poulevoy says much the same: "Undoubtedly the greatest consolation of this life and the greatest resource of our soul is to unite ourselves to Jesus Christ. Yet there is something better, and that is to conform our will to God's will; to be nailed to the Cross with our Lord or to our Lord by His Cross."

Pascal's admirable prayer *for the time of sickness* is well known. It expresses, better than any prayer we have seen, the desire to utilize to the fullest the trials of bad health, which are so painful and serve so well as acts of reparation. We give a quotation from it:

"Do not permit me, dear Lord, to contemplate Thy soul, sorrowful unto death, and Thy body, the prey of death for my sins, without rejoicing in my sufferings of soul and body. For nothing is baser and yet more common with Christians, including myself, than to live lives of pleasure, whilst Thou art sweating blood for the expiation of our sins. Take from me, dear Lord, all sadness that is the fruit of inordinate self-love and give me a sadness like unto Thine. May my sufferings appease Thy anger. I ask of Thee neither life nor death, health nor sickness, but I beseech Thee to dispose of my health, sickness, life, and death, for Thy glory, for my salvation, for the good of the Church and of Thy saints."

Elizabeth Leseur, living in the world, chose as one of her mottoes: "Adoration, *Reparation*, Consolation," and wrote in the same strain as Pascal as follows:

"My God, I am and desire to be ever Thine, in suffering or trial, in aridity or joy, in health or sickness, in life or death. I will one thing only, that Thy will may be done in me, and by me. I pursue and want to pursue one aim only, to procure Thy glory, by the realization of Thy good pleasure in me. I offer myself to Thee to be sacrificed wholly, exteriorly and interiorly. I beseech Thee to dispose of me for Thy service and to aid the souls so dear to Thee; to treat me, in so doing, as the commonest and most lifeless of instruments."

All spiritual writers hold that the most profitable crosses are those which God imposes. St. Francis of Sales writes in his characteristic style: "The best crosses are the heaviest, and the heaviest are those which arouse our greatest repugnance, those which we do not choose, the crosses we find in the streets, and, better still, those we find at home. These are to be preferred to hair shirts, disciplines, fasts, and all other practices of austerity. There is always something of over-nicety in the crosses we choose; because there is something of self in them, they are less crucifying. Humble yourself, therefore, and accept willingly those which are imposed upon you against your will."

But does that mean that all voluntary practices of penance are reserved for the exclusive use of monks and nuns? Many Christians — nay, the greater number — are of this opinion.

There can be no greater mistake. We have cited the passage in which Cardinal Manning exhorts to fidelity to the mortifications enjoined by the Church. To it he adds: "I would go further. Are there any in our days who have the courage to live as the saints lived? We read and admire their lives. We know how austerely and in what poverty they lived. We praise all that and shudder even to think of it. But what are we able to do? Where are our penances? Do we wear the livery of Christ? While seeking to be placed by the world among its votaries, we profess to be the disciples of Jesus Christ!"

In all Christian countries we find this search for comfort and pleasure—we find Catholics who seek to serve God and mammon. In our twentieth century, and especially since the war, the world, including Christ's disciples—at least the greater part—seems to live solely for enjoyment of some kind or other.

Pauline Reynolds, when making a retreat, in her humility wrote as follows: "It is no longer possible to dilate the vessel of my heart destined to overflow with the divine life. The time is over. Yet, by fidelity to grace, I might have cultivated those dispositions which would have obtained for me a thousandfold increase of life throughout eternity. But my will was at fault. *I set limits to trouble I would face.*"

How many Christians, when dying, will have thus to reproach themselves! Yet, if only we put no limits to our generosity in serving God, instead of giving Him a partial fidelity niggardly served out, how greatly could we add to the treasure of merits of the saints!

Cardinal Manning, in his book *The Interior Mission of the Holy Ghost*, explains how we can make reparation. He says: "First, we must promptly follow the inspirations of the divine Spirit. Secondly, we must proportion our fidelity to the measure of His gifts and graces. We must cease acting meanly and burying the talents confided to us; for a thousand talents we ought to give back ten thousand. Finally, we must serve God with great purity of heart, and by this I mean two things: not only avoiding all that might sully the soul, but likewise *sacrificing* whatever tends to usurp the place of God in our souls."

Hence, it is evident, means of making reparation are not wanting. What is, then? Souls prepared to utilize these means; souls ready to combat not only greater sins, but their lesser defects. There are wanting souls, who will devote themselves, not to extraordinary practices, but to the steady, resolute performance of monotonous daily tasks and the generous accomplishment of daily trifles, all of which they offer in reparation. We often aspire to impossible deeds of heroism, but "little things can reveal great love." "It is not so difficult to do great things, they carry us away, but the ordinary duties, insignificant and irksome tasks, exact a measure of self-forgetfulness of which few are capable."[20]

Msgr. de Ségur, with his sound common sense and characteristic subtlety, writes: "Our sanctification is an edifice built up of grains of sand and drops of water. For example, it consists of such trifles as a glance repressed, a word held back, a smile checked, a line unfinished, a souvenir stifled, a welcome letter read only once and that rapidly, a natural reaction boldly restrained, a wearisome bore politely endured, a characteristic exhibition, an outburst of irritation suppressed at once, refraining from a useless purchase, overcoming fits of depression, tempering nature's transports with the thought of God's presence in us, overcoming repugnances: What is all this? Just insignificant trifles in the eyes of men who may not see them, but wonderfully clear to Him Who dwells within us. Here is what we have to watch closely. Here are both the smallest and greatest proofs of fidelity that will draw down torrents of grace upon the soul."

THE POWER OF REPARATION

What miserable creatures we are, seeing that such trifling acts of self-renunciation are the measure of our worth! Yet the fact is undisputed, and no one who has tried to make these acts will contradict Abbé Perrèyve's words, when, speaking from experience, he says: "When we are children, it seems so easy to be a hero or a martyr. But as we advance in life we understand the value of a simple act of virtue and that God alone can give us the strength to accomplish it."

Let us be faithful laborers in performing hidden duties. Who knows but that, during the war, the salvation of some soldier, who fell in the trench or in an assault, was due to his poor suffering grandmother offering her prayers and aches for him. On the battlefield, who can say where the bullet shot by the humblest soldier finds mark?

Do not, dear reader, object: "With what am I to make reparation? How can I, who am so ordinary and insignificant, do this? Like the prophet, I can only say: *A, a, a, et nescio loqui*—'Ah, ah, ah, I know not how to speak' (Jer 1:6). I can only sigh and groan and stammer out my inability. Saints? Yes, they can do something, but what can I do?"

Just as you are, you can do a work of justice, and atone for your infidelities by your fidelity to God. You can do even more, you can not only make up for your own spiritual poverty, but you can offer Him your merits in compensation for the defects and sins of others.

We alone, considered in ourselves, can do absolutely nothing. Granted. But we, *plus* the grace of God, obtained by humility and fervent desires, have a strength and value far exceeding our conception.

With what did Jesus nourish five thousand people in the desert? With five loaves and two fishes. What is the ratio here?

Possibly this saying of one whose whole life was an act of reparation may carry home a deeper conviction: "It is not of gold, silver, or precious stones that our hosts are made, but of a little bread, which is a common substance and of no value." See the humility of her who thus took courage. Her words are true and contain consolation for each one of us.

CHAPTER 8

How Religious Can Make Reparation

SIMONE DENNIEL, A MEMBER of the Congregation of Mary Reparatrix, just quoted, died very young after suffering for a long time from a painful disease, which doubtless God had sent in answer to her vehement desire to suffer. On November 4, 1910, she wrote: "This morning I made a longer thanksgiving after Communion, because I wanted to tell Jesus again and again that I would be His little victim. I thought that perhaps He was seeking for *victims* and that it would be a great work of zeal to instill into souls the desire to be *victims*. Therefore, I will pray and suffer, so that God may increase their number, and raise up true, pure, generous, and holy victims."

It is certain that there are souls who are not satisfied with a modicum of suffering. They have for so long contemplated Christ on the Cross, so deeply realized the miseries of mankind, that they cannot do otherwise than wish to become *victims* with Christ for their neighbor and to give themselves to the utmost as a ransom.

In our ordinary language, the word *victim* has something derogatory about it. We willingly say *sacrifice*, but *victim* has not the same halo. Thus, when we speak of our soldiers' "sacrifices" during the war, a glorious picture presents itself to our minds, but when we refer to the "victims" of the war, the idea of suffering predominates. Yet these two words denote substantially the same notion: there is no sacrifice without a victim. But while *sacrifice* spells enthusiasm, self-surrender, voluntary immolation, *victim* rather suggests the endurance of a slave, bearing involuntarily some suffering which might more justly be styled an injustice or persecution.

It is regrettable that we have to use a word which leaves an unpleasant impression. We ought to employ it knowing exactly what it means. When we speak of a victim, in connection with reparation, it does not mean suffering in spite of oneself, but giving oneself up joyfully. For some souls it is not sufficient to practice resignation, acceptance, and submission. They seek the Cross; they long to find it, and, having succeeded in their quest, with the apostle St. Andrew, they exclaim: *O bona Crux*. They kiss and embrace it. Notwithstanding the repulsion of their whole being, physical, mental, and moral, urged by the love of Christ and of souls, they stretch out their limbs upon the hard, rough beams of the Cross. They offer themselves to be nailed to it. They rejoice to suffer upon the shameful and yet glorious wood.

A fervent religious wrote thus: "Formerly, when our Lord manifested His sufferings to me, I understood Him to say: 'Thou shalt suffer all these.' I knew well that I could never endure His measure of sufferings, but I see that I must suffer in my measure to the full. If I cannot equal His sufferings, I can always fulfill my own." Then she adds: "My chalice is full, how I wish it were larger!"

What a glorious ambition it is to be a victim! It is a strange ideal, so utterly inexplicable, for those who have no conception of true grandeur. "To be a victim! What folly!" they exclaim. No, what supreme wisdom! and how few are capable of understanding its sublimity, because to desire it presupposes so much grace, so many virtues. Yet more souls are capable of this heroism than we might think. All cannot preach, instruct, or write books, but who cannot learn to make the sacrifice of self and to suffer?

Thus to make the complete oblation of self is the most difficult of all vocations, because it calls for the maximum of self-surrender, yet it is not so inaccessible as it seems, for when we have attained the maximum, the rest matters little. Again, only those whom God especially singles out to devote themselves as "victims" can rise to this degree, but the specially chosen are perhaps more numerous than is supposed.

Let me here remind my readers of what has been said previously, as regards the obligation of consulting our director and weighing the obligations of our state of life, besides yielding to the attraction of grace. It is a very great undertaking to offer oneself as a victim: it needs more than a promise, made in a moment of consolation, more than a momentary fervent transport, to face a future that is so formidable. It does not cost us so much merely to *think* of suffering, it is quite another thing to *endure* it. When we kneel in fervent prayer and pain is seen from afar, it stands out in golden letters; looked at nearer, we see they are really written in blood. This does not necessarily involve bodily martyrdom, but it does include a great many trials, which disconcert those who made their oblation with a too ingenuous presumption.

Bearing this in mind, Msgr. d'Hulst states the exact truth when, writing to a secular, he says: "The doctrine of reparation forms the base of *all true interior life*." Hence a truly spiritual life implies the desire to live as a victim, normally a wish, more or less accentuated, to be a sacrifice (host). This is as true of the inner life outside the religious orders as of that within them.

As we have already pointed out, it is in religious orders — more especially in those whose one object is reparation — that we generally find the call to be a victim in its normal, though not its only, center. There may be fervent souls, living in the world, leading apparently a wholly secular life, who are also deeply committed to a life of reparation.

Msgr. d'Hulst's correspondent was one of these privileged Christians. In three letters of direction written by him between 1880 and 1885, he summarizes his views on reparation. He says to her, in a letter dated November 19, 1880: "There is so much to atone for, even — and above all — in the sanctuary and the cloister. God awaits some compensation from those who have received very special graces and profited by them. How grievous are these scandals! Only the thought of reparation can lessen their bitterness. In taking upon ourselves expiation, we resemble Him of Whom it is said: *Vere languores nostros ipse tulit* (Is 53:4). If we were deeply penetrated by this thought, without binding ourselves to do great penances, should we not at least cheerfully accept the vexations and bitterness of life?"

He then goes on to explain in detail how reparation can be made: "We must make atonement by the tears of our heart, by fidelity, patience, deep piety, and love. We must offer our reparation through the intermediary of Mary and of the saints, offering God all their merits, their virtues, their love. We must make reparation by our sufferings, by accepting cheerfully our impotence, spiritual darkness, anguish, weariness, and heaviness of soul. When overtaken by these, let us say: 'It is well. I am ready to bear it; the measure is not overflowing. It is better so, better that I should serve as the wood of the holocaust. If I cannot be the priest who sacrifices, nor the victim, I can be the dead wood, burnt by another, destroyed for the glory of God.'"

Holocaust! This is the limit, there is nothing beyond. A holocaust implies a sacrifice, not a restricted offering, but a total donation, a complete sacrifice, in which the victim is wholly destroyed.

Of all the acts of religion, the holocaust is the most perfect sacrifice, the one that is most glorious for God and meritorious for man, because it is the most significant testimony that man can render to God's Sovereign Majesty, the most solemn protestation of His complete dependence upon the absolute power of God.

Père Ramière remarks: "Words are only too often mere sounds pronounced by our lips. God hears only those prayers which come from the heart, and though their language is more sincere than that of the lips, it is nevertheless liable to illusion. True sacrifice consists in the creature giving up self to destruction in honor of God as Creator. Is not this the most perfect way of confessing that God is the Principle of his life, the Supreme Arbitrator of his destiny?

"Sacrifice is not only the witness of sentiments, words, or actions, it is the testimony of death." When sacrifice reaches the limit of the holocaust, it can go no further. Man can offer no more to his Creator. There is nothing beyond total self-immolation.

The great difficulty, however, is not so much giving oneself unreservedly once for all and all at once, so to say, but after having made this wholesale sacrifice, not to retract in detail from the oblation thus made. The practice of making rapines in the holocaust is traditional in the history of the human race, even as regards those who excel in virtue and strength of will. God allows our self-love to assert itself, so that we may always have numerous occasions of meriting. It would be, surely, too easy, too convenient, if it sufficed to make our sacrifice once for all. Over and over again we have to renew this oblation of ourselves and each time integrally. It is this total donation that constitutes our sacrifice and transforms it into a holocaust.

Practically this amounts to abandoning ourselves to God's good pleasure, in imitation of our Blessed Lord, who said: "My meat is to do the will of Him that sent Me, that I may perfect His work" (Jn 4:34).

Bossuet in his discourse on *Surrender to God* has some beautiful thoughts on this subject, of which we will cite a few:

"Help me to make this act of abandon, my God, so simple and yet so comprehensive because it gives Thee all that I am, and unites me to all that Thou art.

"This act of self-abandonment includes my whole life, not merely that portion which I pass here upon earth as a captive in exile, but likewise my life in eternity. I place my will in Thy hands, I give back to Thee my liberty of action, Thy gift. I have given all to Thee, keeping back nothing. Man can do no more."

By this act of abandonment to the will of God, we do not remain inactive; on the contrary, we are all the more active since we are more under the impulse of the Spirit and become more energetic in serving God.

Self-abandonment to God, as Bossuet explains it, is therefore something totally different from Quietism. In this little work, we have frequently quoted him as an additional witness to the orthodoxy of its teaching.

This act of self-oblation further includes such acts as the subjoined. Never doing agreeable things for the pleasure we find in them, but for God. When a choice of two actions presents itself, to choose the more unpleasant. Since Jesus can no longer suffer, to give Him our sufferings even as the sacramental elements give Him their form and appearances. To let Him substitute our sufferings (since He can no longer suffer) for His, so as to satisfy the ardent desire of His soul to offer sufferings for the glory of the Blessed Trinity and the salvation of souls. To endeavor to become "*Jesus*" under the appearances of "us."[21] Within the limits of discretion and obedience to desire and seek mortification in the little details of life, as a preparation for greater sufferings, should it please God to impose them.

Such are the sublime aspirations of some privileged souls. Joyfully they endeavor to live up to this ideal, each according to her special spiritual attraction and distinctive form of piety.

A word in passing on the "Heroic Act" may fittingly find place here. Some devout Christians make the oblation of all their merits to be applied just as God thinks fit, or for the deliverance of souls from purgatory. They offer all the indulgences they may gain, and all that may be gained for their intention after their decease, for the release of the holy souls.

Another generous act is to make a vow always to do that which is most perfect. Those who make this vow should have sound common sense, a well-balanced judgment, and the sanction of obedience. Otherwise, it might be a fruitful source of scruples and eccentric actions. Here, more than anywhere, souls need "a mind that calculates and a heart that does not calculate." Both are necessary, but the latter is a *sine qua non*.

Others, again, go so far as to engage themselves by a solemn vow to live as victims of reparation. In the Constitutions of the Benedictines of Perpetual Adoration, which have received the approbation of the Holy See, we read: *Voveo et promitto ... omni studio servare perpetuam Sanctissimi Sacramenti altaris adorationem et cultum, uti victima gloriæ ipsius immolata*[22]—"I vow and promise with all diligence to keep up the perpetual adoration and worship of the most Holy Sacrament of the Altar, as a victim immolated to its glory." Hence, this solemn consecration as victim for the glory of God has the formal approbation of the Church. Pius X, by a decree dated December 16th, 1908, and a brief of July, 1909, accorded a monthly indulgence to those priests who, under given conditions, take a vow as priests to make reparation.

But vows of this kind are as difficult to keep as the vow always to choose the most perfect line of action, which the Church speaks of as *arduum* and *arduissimum* in the office for the feasts of St. Andrew Avellino and St. Jane de Chantal respectively. Whence it is clear neither is to be recommended, nor made without wisdom and discretion, prudence and authorization. These are absolutely necessary conditions.

We do not propose to explain this vow of reparation in detail, we leave it to those skilled directors to whom it more particularly appertains and who can deal with it competently. Hence, we pass it over with a brief explanation of the foundation and subject matter of this vow.

Those who desire to make this solemn promise must commence by defining what they intend it to include. These promises may embrace various degrees, but, speaking generally, they can be divided into two classes. The first comprehends all those sufferings which are brought about *by the ordinary providence of God*—sufferings which He has foreordained from eternity. Those who accept these willingly are really "victims" in the hands of God, and they offer Him a very perfect oblation.

Secondly, those fervent souls—not content with these ordinary sacrifices, and desiring to immolate themselves more completely—who beseech God to send them additional sufferings, *as a supplement to the former*. These include sufferings of body, mind, and soul, or even a premature death.

How far is this second and higher degree (1) possible, (2) praiseworthy? These questions must be discussed with extreme caution and great attention, for in such a delicate matter there is a real danger of illusions. As great generosity may lead to temerity, we must exercise all the more prudence and apply more rigorously the rules for "the discernment of spirits."

Of course, it is not necessary to make either of these vows in order to lead a life of reparation. They may crown such a life, but are not necessarily its foundation. They mark a maximum, something, as it were, over the line.

It is a great victory for God that there are souls in this world who desire sufferings with as much avidity as the greater number of men seek pleasures. It seems as though God rejoices in the fact of their existence, by fulfilling willingly their hearts' desires. For He Himself has given them this thirst. When God wants to fill a heart, He begins by emptying it. Whereas all around them have no room within for such yearnings, they are tormented with a thirst to satisfy them to infinity.

First of all, they cannot let our Lord suffer alone upon the Cross, they must alleviate His sufferings by sharing them. They long to wipe His bloodstained brow, to expiate the blows of the hammer when the nails were driven into

His sacred feet and hands, the purple furrows of the lash, by their voluntary and loving oblation. The back of Christ's Cross is empty; there they will seek to be nailed, eager for one thing only, to be crucified in His exact likeness.

They take the advice of St. Catherine of Siena to the letter, which is as follows: "Let the tree of the Cross be planted in your heart and in your soul. Become like unto Jesus Crucified. Hide yourself in His sacred wounds, bathe yourself in the blood of Jesus Crucified, permeate and clothe yourself with Jesus Crucified, satiate yourself with opprobrium in suffering for the love of Jesus Crucified."

A saintly soul, whose Life will, we trust, soon be published, made this candid avowal to her director. She wrote: "We would like sometimes to sing the mercies of the Lord, be it ever so little, but this poor lyre vibrates too much, owing to the density of the materials of which it is made: I can scarcely make any use of it. I began to write to you a few days ago, but was obliged to stop. The first note gave out such a volume of sound, that a second would have snapped the cord.

"My body is too small for my soul and my heart cannot contain my love for Him. ... I can rarely speak as openly with you as I have done this evening, and I have only been able to do so by looking away from Him."

It is related of a religious that, by a special grace of God, she was so overcome with sorrow at the thought of our Lord on the Cross, that she had made a resolution not to look at the crucifix. It chanced that, in order to go to the refectory, she had to pass by a large crucifix fastened to the wall. One day she raised her eyes to it, and, contemplating the bleeding wounds, fell fainting to the ground.

"Exaltation! sensationalism!" you exclaim. Be it so. But, after all, which is most extraordinary? The one who cannot look at the Cross without suffering, or all who contemplate it without feeling any grief whatever. Unlike us, saints cannot look upon the divine immolation with indifference. Those strange beings, saints, suffer when they see our Lord suffer. Alphonsus Rodriguez, a saintly Jesuit lay brother, wrote: "It seems to me that were this suffering of compassion to be prolonged, no form of torment, however horrible, could be compared with it, for this depth of sorrow of soul resembles that of our Lord in Gethsemane, when He prayed, saying: 'My soul is sorrowful, even unto death' (Mt 26:38). It was then that He sweated blood." This holy porter of the College of Majorca offered himself to endure all possible sufferings, even those of the lost, in order to obtain from God that men might cease to offend Him and that no soul might henceforth be lost.

In the *Acta Sanctorum* in the Life of St. Bridget of Sweden, whose feast is kept on October 8th, we read as follows: "When very young, she heard a sermon on the Passion. She was so impressed by it that she imprinted these sorrowful scenes upon the tablet of her heart. The following night she had a vision of our Lord upon the Cross and He said to her: 'This is the treatment I have received.' With her childish simplicity, she asked: 'Lord, who has done that to you?' Jesus replied: 'All those who despise Me and are insensible to My love.' From this moment, St. Bridget was so touched by the Passion of our Savior that she could not help thinking of it continually, always shedding bitter tears over Jesus' sufferings."

This exterior proof of sympathy with our Lord's sorrows is a special gift of God, one of His choicest. Nevertheless, this does not cancel what we said above — namely, that the total abstention from all outward tokens of sympathy proves great indifference and inconceivable ingratitude on the part of men.

If only the Crucifixion of Jesus did some good! He is there, the divine Mediator, suspended between heaven and earth, so mangled, so suffering, and so stupendously ignored.

How can we furnish the tribute of glory which is due to God and refused Him by man? By loving Him?

Alas! a poor human word, and it represents a still poorer thing. With what can we love? With our wretched human heart? For the heart of man to love God seems a derision, mere irony. That which is the weakest, can it love that which is greatest? Can we, so ungenerous, love Him who has given Himself without measure? His generosity is proved by the manger, the Cross, Holy Mass, the Sacraments, the Church. He gives all; how can we who limit and begrudge our gifts offer Him anything? Can we, whose love is feeble, so unworthy of the name, love Him who is Love itself? No, Lord, we cannot compete with Thee.

What a conflict! To enter the lists with one who wields the infinite, this thought inevitably rends and tortures the soul. We long to give and have not the wherewithal. We would fain give much and our hands are empty. To Him who is All, we must ever give so little.

Assuredly, it is not necessary to possess much in order to give much. He who gives all he possesses, however little it be, certainly gives much.

Yet, herein is another source of spiritual anguish: a continual torment, because one is conscious that one does not give wholly to God the little one has. We know ourselves and cannot but admit our daily shortcomings. These may be trifles, but still how hateful it is to show the least lack of feeling in one's love of God. Hence, what should lessen her suffering only increases it. One longs to console the Master, by offering oneself wholly to Him, but is conscious of numerous evasions, acts of meanness and self-love. St. Francis of Sales wittily tells us we shall not get rid of this feeling until a quarter of an hour after death. It is just this that overwhelms one. We have to serve God, Who merits all; we have so little to give Him and this little is not fully given up.

God torments saints with this constant anguish. Their desires continually grow stronger, and He only puts this consuming flame in their hearts that He may contemplate their great magnanimity with pleasure, amidst all the pettinesses that He hates.

Sister Teresa of the Infant Jesus, once said to our Lord: "I offer myself to Thee as a victim, a holocaust to Thy merciful love, that I may live in an act of perfect love. I pray Thee, consume me unceasingly; let the torrents of infinite tenderness that overflow Thy soul pass into mine, so that I may be a martyr of love, O my God. ... O, my Beloved, with every beat of my heart, I renew this offering to Thee an infinite number of times, until earth's shadows shall have passed away and face-to-face in eternity I can tell Thee my love."

In a meditation in which St. Mary Magdalene de Pazzi received great spiritual illumination from God, she speaks thus of St. Aloysius Gonzaga: "Who can ever explain the priceless value of interior acts and the reward they merit! There is no comparison between what appears without and what takes place within. St. Aloysius, all his life long, thirsted after the interior inspirations which the Word breathed into his soul. He was an unknown martyr, for all who love Thee, my God, all who know how great and infinitely lovable Thou art, suffer a cruel martyrdom on seeing that they do not love Thee as they would wish, and that instead of loving Thee, so many continually offend Thee."

It would be some consolation to those who thirst for God, at last to find Him and hold Him in a loving embrace. ... But alas! as we follow after God, He hides Himself. True, there is the Holy Eucharist, but the Real Presence does not last always; it is so mysterious: *Visus, tactus, gustus, in te fallitur.*[23] There is sanctifying grace, but the continual presence of God in the soul does not always ensure the presence of the soul in herself.

We are continually away from ourselves. Our frequent and trivial daily cares carry us far from this precious center where, by sanctifying grace, "The Three" — Father, Son, and Holy Ghost — always dwell. God is present *in* us: we are there not at all — or so little.

Then there is prayer, but even so we must be content with faith, while we desire possession, with the reflection instead of the gift, with the image in the "glass" instead of the "face-to-face" (see 1 Cor 13:12).

We want to be like unto Jesus, and yet how utterly far away He seems, how hidden, how hard to realize. Then we must add those terrible spiritual trials of aridity, when the divine Master seems so far off and dim that we can scarcely recognize Him and cry out with the apostles on the lake: *Phantasma est!*—"It is an apparition" (Mt 14:26).

Yet Jesus knows we have left all to follow Him. Marie de la Bouillerie, who became a religious of the Congregation of the Sacred Heart, speaking of her mother, said: "I will never leave her for a man." But the religious leaves her mother because she knows that Jesus was more than man. She says resolutely to Him: "I will follow Thee. Where dwellest Thou?" He replies: "Wilt thou follow Me? Come then." She sets out for the promised land, knowing that the road is long, and that it leads through the desert. What matters it? After a weary march, she thinks she has reached her Master's abode, the King's palace—she knocks at the door like the child who once clambered up on to the altar, knocked at the door of the tabernacle, and called out: "Lord, are You there?" and got no answer from within. So for her, too, the Tabernacle door remains closed. God does not reveal Himself.

Deus absconditus—"He is a hidden God" (Is 45:15). He crucifies and remains hidden, unspeakably mysterious and unapproachable! There we stay knowing that He is within and could open, but prefers to wait. Thus was it with St.

Mary Magdalene at the tomb on Easter morning. She sets out at dawn with her humble offering, a few spices—it is all she can offer—and she hurries on her mission of love. She reaches the garden and enters the tomb. The tomb is empty—there is an angel, the grave clothes, some traces of Him—but not the Master! Yet "He" is the One she wants; not just the word of an angel, but a word from Him, His own lips; not merely a relic of His showing He was there just now; but *Him*, there in fact, now, plain to all of us. "Art Thou here, O Lord?" He is not far off. He is always close to those that seek Him.

"Thou wouldst not seek Me, hadst thou not already found Me." Pascal places these words on our Lord's lips, and they express a great truth. Those who seek in earnest and cry out: "Lord, where art Thou?" are no longer on the way—they have reached the end. While Mary Magdalene was asking for Him, the Master was there, standing in front of her. It was He Himself though He showed Himself as usual, in a disguise, as a gardener, and she did not recognize Him: "Tell me where He is. Wherever He is, let me go to find Him."

If the Lord manifested Himself openly, He would satisfy the soul's desire, but not His own. He takes pleasure in the spiritual thirst of fervent souls. He is like a mother who hides for her child to find her. "God desires nothing so much as to be desired," as St. Augustine says. That is why His wise action tortures us, but affords Him such pleasure. *Deus absconditus.* God hides Himself, and this is why His lovers suffer so much.

Religious have left all for God, that they may be united with Him and yet, in spite of all their desires and efforts, they find they can never possess Him and be wholly His. With the spouse in the Canticles, they exclaim: *Fasciculus myrrhæ Dilectus meus*—"A bundle of myrrh is my Beloved" (1:12). In the bitterness of their myrrh, God finds a sweet perfume of the greatest love.

Thus He could not long withstand Mary Magdalene's entreaties. Familiarly, as of old, He pronounces her name, "Mary!" Nor can He resist souls that seek Him. At times, He allows them to see Him as in a flash. They feel that they need only throw themselves at His feet, and stretch out their hands to lay hold of Him forever! Then He speaks: *Noli me tangere* (Jn 20:17). On hearing these words, "Touch Me not," their sorrow is at its sharpest. Is this to be the sole reward of their love? Has it counted for no more? "Lord, take away my heart's desire, or have mercy on me," they cry. But then especially He refuses to treat them otherwise. He wishes to deepen their inward yearnings, and hence He bids them wait with patience, and veils the reality of mercy under the form of ruthlessness. It is related that He once said to Pauline Reynolds: "My hour has not yet come. Be patient, in a short time you will see Me." "Do You speak thus to a soul that loves?" she answered; to which our Lord replied: "Yes, I speak thus to one who loves because I love. Trust Me implicitly."

Amidst the sufferings which spring from a soul's insatiable desire to give something, even much, to God, He provides her with means of showing herself more equal to her high ideals. That self-sacrifice spells suffering, the soul is convinced. She is unhappy precisely because her offering to God has cost too little.

Then, God sends great crosses, such as aridity, illness, false friends, persecution, failures, and many other kinds of excruciating suffering. Our Lord is never at a loss for crosses. His workshop is full of them. At Nazareth, He apparently spent all His time making crosses of various sizes and kinds of wood.

This is how God acts: to slake a soul's thirst for sacrifice He sends suffering. He fills the full cup of suffering by making it overflow, and the fresh influx of bitterness results in the greatest happiness. Were we not accustomed to be so continually baffled by God's mysterious dealings with man, how amazed we should be at the strange paradox, by which our loving God imposes such great sufferings on those who are generous enough to offer themselves as holocausts.

St. Lydwine, as we have previously said, exclaimed in the midst of her pain: "Do not pity me, I am happy," and all who walk in her footsteps reecho her sentiments. Her biographer takes these words as his text in one of the finest passages ever written on suffering. This is the substance of his remarks: Victims suffer most of all and yet are the happiest of all. To offer oneself for a holocaust is to offer oneself for happiness, for Jesus owes it to Himself to repay in peace and joy that which has been sacrificed for Him so generously. This is the experience of all eminent self-immolators. God compensates them so abundantly for their sacrifices that they exclaim: "Dear Lord, what a blundering bargain. I meant to suffer and expiate, and I have nothing but happiness." A soul says to Jesus: "Let me be nailed to Thy Cross by Thee, O Lord." Jesus grants the petition. He drives in the nails; then seeing the blood flow and the victim break down, His heart breaks: He cannot go on. He stops, draws near, and fills the void wrought by suffering with joy, so that the soul begs to be spared joy, as earnestly as others beg to be spared sorrow. Yet she goes on suffering, but her suffering is her happiness, or rather, while still feeling her suffering, it is so full of divine gladness that she would not be relieved of the suffering for anything in the world. She must have it to provide fuel for the fire of sacrifice; and God trains the soul with alternate gladness and grief, each making the way for the other. Yet, after all, suffering is swallowed up in joy; and the soul's unstifled sobs break forth like "hymns," as Bauthier finely says.

Abbé Perrèyve, a writer who excels in understanding and explaining the paradox of suffering and joy intermingling or balancing one with the other, writes: "How comes it, Lord, that no sooner have I set out on the way of the Cross than I hear such sweet consoling words?" No sooner has Jesus said, "If any one will come after Me, let him take up his cross," than He adds, "My yoke is sweet and My burden is light" (Mt 16:24; 11:30). The Abbé continues: "I have only just commenced my sacrifice when Thou givest me consolation; no sooner have I taken up my cross than I feel Thy divine hand lessening its weight.

"O Jesus, Thou Who orderest the sacrifices that are needed, and yet dost ever diminish their pain by Thy tender love, Thou dost command us to renounce self, and when we practice detachment from creatures, Thou givest us far more treasures than we have given up. Thou commandest us to take up our cross daily, if we would follow Thee, and then dost exchange it for a yoke that is sweet and a burden that is light. Thou art often so pleased with the least proof of our goodwill, and dost reward our feeble efforts with unutterable consolations. Henceforth, I will not be afraid of Thee nor of Thy gospel, nor will I tremble on hearing the word *cross*. I know that the Cross contains the secret of all great consolations; and real succor in the pathway of life, where inevitably we must suffer. I draw near with confidence to the Cross; kneeling before it, I would find fresh graces of strength and patience by meditating on Thy Passion. Dear generous Master, do not refuse me this gift; receive me in the ranks of Thy faithful disciples, who, following Thee even to Calvary, find courage to endure their trials, and grace to exchange earth's bitter sorrows for boundless wealth."

Can we do better than close this chapter with such a beautiful, fervent, confiding, and humble prayer?

Humility is the characteristic that finally sets its hallowing seal upon the true spirit of reparation. All who resolve to devote themselves with Christ, to redeem the world by suffering, tremble as they do so, knowing their utter helplessness. They know that, left to themselves, the least touch of suffering would put them to flight. Those who offer themselves with the wine of the sacrifice know well that they are but drops of water. It is ever the most generous who realize most fully the utter insignificance of their gifts.

CONCLUSION

WE HAVE NOT TRIED to write an exhaustive or learned treatise on reparation, but to explain simply the theological and dogmatic foundation upon which it rests, and the proper place in Christian life and thought of this Ideal.

At the present moment, many seem to be drawn toward it, but, because they do not clearly understand in what it consists, they hesitate, fumble about, give up, or go off on the wrong scent. These few pages seek to awaken some souls, and to help those already awake, but needing enlightenment, by sketching out the first principles.

Undoubtedly, in such a matter, a monograph or a living example is better than a booklet. This is why we have so frequently quoted from *Lives*. However, a brief outline of the theory may be useful and serve as an attraction and a landmark. Afterward, the perusal of deeper treatises, the advice of a skilled director, and the grace of the Holy Spirit may complete the work of enlightenment, conviction, and stimulation.

During the recent war, along the roads leading to the battlefront, here and there, you came across noticeboards, on which were roughly scrawled names of places and arrows. They pointed the way to some definite goal. These pages are simply meant to say: To Self-Sacrifice — "Follow the Way of Reparation." They tell you the road to the goal from afar, not what you will find when you get there.

Just as only those who lived in the trenches during the war know what kind of life our soldiers lived, and all that happened there, and alone can speak of it with authority, whether or no they are listened to or believed in, so only those who have been taught by God, either by personal experience or by contact with privileged souls, can adequately instruct others in the complete overthrow of self-love, in self-annihilation, and in the blood-dyed festivities of the total giving over of self to God.

This accounts for the particular form of this book, for its incomplete and cursory nature. It does not befit us to sound depths which God reserves to Himself, to search into "the King's secret" and explain how He communicates Himself to those whom He calls to give up all for Him. To do that presupposes authority, practical asceticism, and mystical experience, and something else which the author does not possess. A blind man does not describe light.

We are only too conscious of how far this little book falls short of expectation. But, however imperfect this modest work be, God can utilize it for His glory, if He so wills.

CONCLUSION

Sometimes He makes use of the most inadequate means to produce the results He desires.

In September 1917, during the war, two soldiers were on leave at Hersin-Coupigny in Pas-de-Calais. They decided to return to their native village to look for their savings, which they had buried before leaving for the campaign. One found his money, the other nothing whatever. Before returning, they went to see their old church. Alas! it was in ruins, only a cast-iron crucifix that had been fastened to the wall remained erect. One of the soldiers reverently kissed it, in presence of a group of Canadian comrades who applauded heartily. Then, turning to his companion, he said: "You have found your treasure and now I have found mine. I will take it away." They took the heavy cross, carried it over the beaten tracks, and through underground passages, and at last, covered with mud and dripping with perspiration, they reached Hersin and there placed the cross of their church in safety.

To *find* the Cross, not that of a church in ruins and among the debris, but our Lord's Cross planted on Calvary, might seem an easy task. Yet it is not. As Msgr. d'Hulst truthfully says when speaking of the feast of the Finding of the Holy Cross: "It is a great discovery. For a long time we have had thieves' crosses that dishonor, but the great revelation is the Cross of Jesus. How many souls have yet to find it!"

Yes, souls must first find the Cross, but this does not suffice. They must clasp the Cross in their arms. The Canadians applauded their brave comrade. The world will not understand the true Christian's love of the Cross. What matters it?

Having taken up their Cross, they must place it resolutely upon their shoulders. They will find their narrow paths, their subterranean passages, and obstacles which will make them stumble and fall. The path is rough, the road long. They will often be tempted to throw down their burden, to rid themselves of its weight and ease their aching limbs. Then the Master asks: "Wilt thou leave Me there? Is there no one who will, like Simon and Veronica, take charge of My Cross and help Me?" Will none come forward? Are our Master's words true?

One day, while Blessed Angela of Foligno was hearing Mass, our Lord gave her a great realization of the sufferings of Jesus on the Cross. She writes: "I heard Him bless the unselfish who imitated His Passion and took pity on Him. He said: 'May the hand of My Father bless you, who have shared and wept over My Passion. You whom I have ransomed from hell by My terrible sufferings have taken pity on Me. May His blessing rest on the faithful who have remembered My Passion and kept the memory of it in their hearts, for they have offered to their Lord in His desolation the sacred hospitality of their love.

"'I was naked upon the Cross, I hungered and thirsted, and you pitied Me. I bless you for your work of mercy. In your last moments, I will welcome you, saying: "Come, ye blessed of My Father, for I hungered and you dealt out to Me the bread of your compassion." If, hanging upon the Cross, I prayed for My executioners, what shall I say of you who have served Me so faithfully when I come in glory to judge the world? I cannot express the love I feel for all hearts full of pity.'"

CONCLUSION

More than ever, at the present time, Jesus asks for "devoted souls, ready to imitate His Passion and to pity Him."

May the divine Master lead at least a few of the readers of these pages to enroll themselves in the cohort of the "devoted," and grant them the generous desire to join the "pitiful in heart."

Who is willing?

"Here am I, Lord."

APPENDIX A
PRAYERS FOR MAKING REPARATION

INDULGENCED PRAYERS FROM THE "RACCOLTA"

Prayer to Jesus Our Redeemer[24]

O Jesus, Son of the living God, my Savior and Redeemer, behold us prostrate at Thy feet. We beg pardon, and make this act of reparation for all the blasphemies uttered against Thy holy name, for all the outrages committed against Thee in the most Holy Sacrament of the Altar, for all irreverence shown to Thy most blessed and immaculate Mother, and for all the calumnies spoken against Thy Spouse, our holy mother, the Catholic Church. O Jesus, who didst say: "Whatever you shall ask the Father in My name, that I will do" (Jn 14:13), we pray and beseech Thee for our brethren who are living in danger of sin, that Thou wouldst preserve them from the seductions of apostasy. Save them who stand over the abyss; give them light and knowledge of the truth, power and strength in the conflict against evil, and perseverance in faith and active charity. And therefore, most merciful Jesus, do we pray to the Father in Thy name, with Whom Thou livest and reignest, in the unity of the Holy Spirit, world without end. Amen.

Acts of Adoration and Reparation[25]

I

I adore Thee, my Jesus, in the Blessed Sacrament; I acknowledge Thee, true God and true Man. By this act of adoration, I intend to make Thee reparation for the coldness of so many of Thy people, who pass before Thy churches, nay, before Thy very tabernacle, where hour after hour Thou dost deign to dwell in loving impatience to communicate Thyself to Thy faithful, yet do not even bow the knee before Thee, but like the Israelites in the wilderness, seem by their indifference to loathe this heavenly Manna. I offer Thee Thine own most Precious Blood which Thou didst shed from the wound in Thy left foot, in reparation for this hateful coldness, and entering therein, I cry, and will never cease to cry:

Blessed and praised every moment
Be the most Holy and Divine Sacrament!
Pater, Ave, Gloria.

II

I profoundly adore Thee, my Jesus; I acknowledge Thee present in the most Holy Sacrament. By this act of adoration, I would fain make amends for the forgetfulness of so many Christian people, who, when they see Thee go to the poor sick, to be their Strength in their great journey to eternity, leave Thee unescorted, and hardly give Thee even one outward sign of homage. I offer Thee, in reparation for this coldness, that most Precious Blood which Thou didst shed from the wound in Thy right foot, and entering therein, I cry, and will never cease to cry:

    Blessed and praised every moment
    Be the most Holy and Divine Sacrament!
Pater, Ave, Gloria.

III

I profoundly adore Thee, my Jesus, true Bread of life eternal; and by this my act of adoration, I would fain make Thee compensation for all the wounds with which Thy Sacred Heart bleeds daily to see the profanation of those churches wherein Thou dost vouchsafe to abide, beneath the sacramental species, to receive the love and adoration of Thy people. I offer Thee, in reparation for all these irreverences, that most Precious Blood which Thou didst shed from the wound in Thy left hand, and, entering therein, I will ever cry:

    Blessed and praised every moment
    Be the most Holy and Divine Sacrament!
Pater, Ave, Gloria.

IV

I profoundly adore Thee, my Jesus, living Bread come down from heaven; and by this act of adoration, I would fain make amends for all the acts of irreverence which Thy people day by day commit whilst they assist at Holy Mass, in which bloodless Sacrifice Thou dost renew the very Sacrifice which once Thou didst consummate on Calvary for our salvation. I offer Thee, in reparation for all this ingratitude, that most Precious Blood which Thou didst shed from the wound in Thy right hand; and, entering therein, I unite my voice with the voices of the holy angels who adore around Thy throne:

Blessed and praised every moment

Be the most Holy and Divine Sacrament!

Pater, Ave, Gloria.

V

I profoundly adore Thee, my Jesus, true Victim of expiation for our sins; and I offer Thee this act of adoration in compensation for the sacrilegious outrages Thou dost receive from so many of Thy ungrateful people, who dare to draw nigh to Thee and receive Thee in Communion with mortal sin upon their souls. In reparation for these hateful sacrileges, I offer Thee those last drops of Thy most Precious Blood which Thou didst shed from the wound in Thy side; and, entering therein, I approach Thee with acts of adoration, love, and thanksgiving, and, with all holy souls who are devout to Thee in this most Holy Sacrament, I cry:

Blessed and praised every moment

Be the most Holy and Divine Sacrament!

Pater, Ave, Gloria.

"Tantum Ergo"

Tantum ergo Sacramentum	Down in adoration falling,
Veneremur cernui:	Lo! the Sacred Host we hail,
Et antiquum documentum	Lo! o'er ancient forms departing
Novo cedat ritui:	Newer rites of grace prevail;
Præstet fides supplementum	Faith for all defects supplying,
Sensuum defectui.	Where the feeble senses fail.
Genitori, Genitoque	To the Everlasting Father,
Laus et jubilatio,	And the Son Who reigns on high
Salus, honor, virtus, quoque	With the Holy Ghost proceeding
Sit et benedictio:	Forth from Each eternally,
Procedenti ab utroque	Be salvation, honour, blessing,
Compar sit laudatio. Amen.	Might, and endless majesty. Amen.
℣. Panem de cœlo præstitisti eis.	℣. Thou hast given them bread from heaven.
℟. Omne delectamentum in se habentem.	℟. Having within it all sweetness.

Oremus. Deus, qui nobis sub Sacramento mirabili Passionis Tuæ memoriam reliquisti: tribue, quæsumus, ita nos Corporis et Sanguinis Tui Sacra Mysteria venerari, ut redemptionis Tuæ fructum in nobis jugiter sentiamus. Qui vivis et regnas in sæcula sæculorum. Amen.	Let us pray: O God, Who in this wonderful Sacrament left us a memorial of Thy Passion: grant, we implore Thee, that we may so venerate the Sacred Mysteries of Thy Body and Blood, as always to be conscious of the fruit of Thy Redemption. Thou who livest and reignest forever and ever. Amen.

Act of Reparation and Ejaculations[26]

Jesus, my God, my Savior, true God and true Man, in that lowly homage with which the faith itself inspires me, with my whole heart I adore and love Thee in the most august Sacrament of the Altar, in reparation for all the acts of irreverence, profanation, and sacrilege, which I myself may ever have been so unhappy as to have committed, as well as for all such like acts that ever have been done by others, or that may be done in ages yet to come. I adore Thee, my God, not indeed as Thou deservest, nor as much as I am bound to adore, but as far as I am able; and I would that I could adore Thee with all the perfection of which a reasonable creature is capable. Meantime, I purpose now and ever to adore Thee, not only for those Catholics who adore and love Thee not, but also for the conversion of all bad

Christians, and of all heretics, schismatics, Mohammedans, Jews, and idolaters. Jesus, my God, mayest Thou be ever known, adored, loved, and praised every moment, in the most holy and divine Sacrament. Amen.

I adore Thee every moment, O living Bread of heaven, great Sacrament!

Jesus, Heart of Mary, I pray Thee send Thy blessing on my soul.

Holiest Jesu! loving Savior! I give Thee my heart.

Prayer of St. Alphonsus Liguori, to Be Said at a Visit to the Most Holy Sacrament[27]

My Lord Jesus Christ, Who for the love which Thou dost bear men dost remain night and day in this Sacrament, all full of tenderness and love, expecting, inviting, and receiving all those who come to visit Thee; I believe Thee present in the Sacrament of the Altar; I adore Thee in the depths of my own nothingness; and I thank Thee for all the graces which Thou hast granted me, especially for having vouchsafed to bestow Thyself upon me in this Sacrament, for having given me Thy own most holy Mother Mary for my Advocate, and for having invited me to visit Thee in this church. I pay my homage this day to Thy adorable Heart, and I do so for the following three intentions: first, in thanksgiving for this great Gift itself; secondly, as a reparation for all the injuries which Thou hast received from all Thy enemies in this Sacrament; thirdly, by this visit I intend to adore Thee in all those places where Thou, sacramentally present, art least reverenced and most abandoned. My Jesus,

I love Thee with my whole heart. I repent of having so many times heretofore displeased Thy infinite goodness. By Thy grace, I resolve never to offend Thee more for the time to come; and at this present moment, poor sinner as I am, I consecrate myself wholly to Thee. I renounce for myself, and I give to Thee, my will, my affections, my desires, everything that I call my own. From this day forth do Thou with me, and with everything that belongs to me, whatever pleases Thee. I ask Thee only, and I wish only, for Thy holy love, for final perseverance, and the perfect fulfillment of Thy will. I commend to Thee the souls in purgatory, especially those who were most devoted to the most Holy Sacrament, and to Mary most holy. Moreover, I commend to Thee all poor sinners. For this intention, O my dear Savior Jesus, I unite all my affections with the affections of Thy most loving Heart; and thus united, I offer them to Thy eternal Father, and I entreat Him, in Thy name and for Thy love, to accept and answer them.

Seven Offerings, in Reparation for All the Outrages Received by Our Lord in the Precious Blood[28]

I

Eternal Father! I offer Thee the merits of the Precious Blood of Jesus, Thy well-beloved Son, my Savior and my God, for the propagation and exaltation of my dear mother, Thy holy Church; for the safety and prosperity of her visible head, our chief pastor the Bishop of Rome; for the cardinals, bishops, and pastors of souls, and for all the ministers of the sanctuary. *Gloria Patri.*

Blessed and praised forevermore be Jesus, Who hath saved us with His Blood.

II

Eternal Father! I offer Thee the merits of the Precious Blood of Jesus, Thy well-beloved Son, my Savior and my God, for the peace and concord of Catholic kings and princes, for the humiliation of the enemies of our holy Faith, and for the welfare of all Christian people. *Gloria Patri.*

Blessed and praised, and so on.

III

Eternal Father! I offer Thee the merits of the Precious Blood of Jesus, Thy well-beloved Son, my Savior and my God, for the repentance of unbelievers, the uprooting of heresy, and the conversion of sinners. *Gloria Patri.*

Blessed and praised, and so on.

IV

Eternal Father! I offer Thee the merits of the Precious Blood of Jesus, Thy well-beloved Son, my Savior and my God, for all my relations, friends, and enemies; for the poor, the sick, and the afflicted, and for all those for whom Thou, my God, knowest that I ought to pray, or wouldst have me pray. *Gloria Patri.*

Blessed and praised, and so on.

V

Eternal Father! I offer Thee the merits of the Precious Blood of Jesus, Thy well-beloved Son, my Savior and my God, for all who this day are passing to the other life; that Thou wouldst save them from the pains of hell, and admit them quickly to the possession of Thy glory. *Gloria Patri.*

Blessed and praised, and so on.

VI

Eternal Father! I offer Thee the merits of the Precious Blood of Jesus, Thy well-beloved Son, my Savior and my God, for all those who love this great treasure, for those who join with me in adoring it and honoring it, and for those who strive to spread devotion to it. *Gloria Patri.*

Blessed and praised, and so on.

VII

Eternal Father! I offer Thee the merits of the Precious Blood of Jesus, Thy well-beloved Son, my Savior and my God, for all my wants, spiritual and temporal; in suffrage for the holy souls in purgatory, and chiefly for those who were most devout lovers of this Blood, the price of our redemption, and of the sorrows and pains of our dear Mother, most holy Mary. *Gloria Patri.*

Blessed and praised, and so on.

Glory be to the Blood of Jesus, now and forever, and throughout all ages! Amen.

Act of Oblation to Be Made before a Representation of the Sacred Heart[29]

My loving Jesus, out of the grateful love I bear Thee, and to make reparation for my unfaithfulness to grace, I (N. N.) give Thee my heart, and I consecrate myself wholly to Thee; and with Thy help I purpose never to sin again.

Prayer to the Eucharistic Heart[30]

O Eucharistic Heart, O sovereign love of our Lord Jesus, Who hast instituted the august Sacrament, in order to dwell here below with us and to give to our souls Thy Flesh as food and Thy Blood as drink, we confidently trust, O Lord Jesus, in the supreme love which instituted the most Holy Eucharist; and here, in the presence of this Victim, it is just that we should adore, confess, and exalt this love, as the great storehouse of the life of Thy Church. This love is an urgent invitation for us, as though Thou didst say to us: "See how I love you! giving you My Flesh as food, and My Blood as drink; I desire by this union to excite your charity, I desire to unite you to Myself, I desire to effect the transformation of your souls into My crucified Self, I Who am the Bread of eternal life. Give me then your hearts, live in My life, and you shall live in God." We recognize, O Lord, that such is the appeal of Thy Eucharistic Heart, and we thank Thee for it, and we desire earnestly to respond to it. Grant us the grace to be keenly alive to this supreme love, with which, before Thy Passion, Thou didst invite us to receive and feed upon Thy sacred Body. Print deeply on our souls the firm determination to respond faithfully to this invitation. Give us devotion and reverence whereby we may honor and receive worthily the gift of Thy supreme love, and of Thy Eucharistic Heart. Grant that we may thus be able, with Thy grace, to celebrate profitably the remembrance of Thy Passion, to make reparation for our offenses and our coldness, to nourish and increase our love for Thee, and to keep ever living within our hearts this seed of a blessed immortality. Amen.

Act of Reparation[31]

Most glorious Virgin Mary, Mother of God, and our Mother, look with pity upon us poor sinners, who, afflicted with so many miseries surrounding us in this life, feel ourselves cut to the heart by the many horrible insults and blasphemies which we are often constrained to hear uttered against thee, O immaculate Virgin. Oh, how these impious sayings offend the infinite Majesty of God, and Jesus Christ His only begotten Son! How they provoke His anger, and give us cause to fear the terrible effects of His vengeance! If the sacrifice of our lives could avail against such outrages and blasphemies, very willingly would we make it, for we desire, most holy Mother, to love and honor thee with all our hearts, such being the will of God. And just because we love thee, we will do whatever lies in our power to make thee loved and honored by all. And do thou, Mother of pity, supreme consoler of the afflicted, accept this act of reparation offered to thee, in our name and in the name of all our families, and on behalf of those who, not knowing what they say, impiously blaspheme thee; that so, by obtaining from God their conversion, thy glorious compassion, thy power, and thy great mercy may become more manifest, and they too may join with us in proclaiming thee blessed amongst women, the immaculate Virgin, the most compassionate Mother of God. Ave Maria *thrice*.

Reparation for Blasphemy against Our Lady[32]

O Mary, bless this house, where thy name is ever held in benediction. All glory to Mary ever immaculate, ever Virgin, blessed among women, the Mother of our Lord Jesus Christ, Queen of paradise.

Temperance Pledge[33]

O God, my Father, to show my love for Thee, to make reparation to Thy wounded honor, to obtain the salvation of souls, I firmly purpose to take this day neither wine, nor beer, nor any intoxicating drink.

I offer Thee this act of mortification in union with the sacrifice of Thy Son Jesus Christ, Who daily offers Himself a Victim on the altar for Thy greater glory. Amen.

Prayer for the Conversion of Freemasons[34]

O Lord Jesus Christ, Who showest forth Thy omnipotence most manifestly when Thou sparest and hast compassion; Thou Who didst say, "Pray for those who persecute and calumniate you" (Mt 5:44), we implore the clemency of Thy Sacred Heart on behalf of souls, made in the image of God, but most miserably deceived by the treacherous snares of Freemasons, and going more and more astray in the way of perdition. Let not the Church, Thy Spouse, any longer be oppressed by them; but, appeased by the intercession of the Blessed Virgin Thy Mother and the prayers of the just, be mindful of Thy infinite mercy; and, disregarding their perversity, cause these very men to return to Thee, that they may bring consolation to the Church by a most abundant penance, make reparation for their misdeeds, and secure for themselves a glorious eternity; Who livest and reignest world without end. Amen.

OTHER PRAYERS

Act of Reparation for Blasphemy
Blessed be God.
Blessed be His holy name.
Blessed be Jesus Christ, true God and true Man.
Blessed be the name of Jesus.
Blessed be Jesus in the most Holy Sacrament of the Altar.
Blessed be the great Mother of God, Mary most holy.
Blessed be her holy and Immaculate Conception.
Blessed be the name of Mary, Virgin and Mother.
Blessed be God in His angels and in His saints.

Act of Reparation to the Sacred Heart
O Jesus, only Son of the living God, Who, by an incomprehensible effect of Thy love, wast pleased to be made Man, to be born in a stable, to live amidst labors and sufferings, to

die upon a Cross, and to leave us, as a perpetual pledge of Thy tenderness, Thine own Body and Blood for the nourishment of our souls, in the ineffable Sacrament of the Eucharist: Thou beholdest at Thy feet a criminal covered with confusion, who comes, in the spirit of union with all the associates in the adoration of Thy divine Heart, humbly to confess his ingratitude, his iniquities, and those of all other men, that he may make reparation for them as far as in him lies.

Alas! O loving Jesus, we have sinned against heaven and before Thee. What hath Thy most Sacred Heart not suffered on our part in the course of Thy sacred life, in Thy bitter Passion, and from the moment that Thou hast dwelt amongst us in the Sacrament of Thy love! O with how much bitterness, opprobrium, and grief have we deluged Thy divine Heart! Pardon; mercy; O adorable Heart of Jesus! mercy for me, mercy for all men, and for our land in particular!

I detest, with all the sincerity of my soul, and with the most profound and bitter grief, everything which hath ever offended Thee in myself or in others; I detest it for the love Thou deservest, and which is supremely due unto Thee. O that I could efface with my tears, and wash away with my blood, the injuries which we have done unto Thee. O that I could repay Thee, by my repentance, by my works, and by my love, all the glory, honor, and satisfaction of which Thou hast been robbed by the injuries and outrages that have been committed against Thee! Accept at least the earnest desire with which Thou inspirest me.

Vouchsafe, O Heart infinitely rich in mercy, to light again in my heart and that of all men the sacred fire which

Thou camest to kindle upon the earth. Let it purify them, let it inflame them, let it make of them one heart with Thy Heart. Pour down, I beseech Thee, Thy most precious and abundant benedictions on Thy holy Church, and those who govern it; on this diocese, on this region, and on all those who are united with us in devotion to Thy Sacred Heart. O Heart of Jesus, live, reign in all hearts, for time and for eternity. Amen.

Reparation of Honor to the Sacred Heart

O most amiable and adorable Heart of Jesus! Center of all hearts, glowing with charity, and inflamed with zeal for the interest of Thy Father and the salvation of mankind; O Heart, ever sensible of our misery, and ever ready to redress our evils; the real Victim of love in the Holy Eucharist, and a propitiatory Sacrifice for sin on the altar of the Cross! seeing that the generality of Christians make no other return for these Thy mercies, than contempt for Thy favors, forgetfulness of their own obligations, and ingratitude to the best of benefactors; is it not just that we Thy servants, penetrated with the deepest sense of such indignities, should, as far as in our power, make a due and satisfactory reparation of honor to Thy most sacred Majesty? Prostrate, therefore, in body, and humbled in mind, before heaven and earth, we solemnly declare our utter detestation and abhorrence of such conduct. Inexpressible, we know, was the bitterness which the multitude of our sins brought on Thy tender Heart; insufferable the weight of our iniquities, which pressed Thy face to the earth in the Garden of Olives; and insurmountable Thy anguish, when expiring with love, grief, and agony, on Mount Calvary, in Thy last breath Thou wouldst reclaim sinners to their duty and repentance. This we know, O dear Redeemer! and would most willingly redress these Thy sufferings by our own, or share with Thee in Thine!

O merciful Jesus! ever present on our altars, and with a Heart open to receive all who labor and are burdened! O adorable Heart of Jesus, Source of true contrition, impart to our hearts the true spirit of penance, and to our eyes a fountain of tears, that we may bewail our sins, and the sins of the world. Pardon, divine Jesus! all the injuries and outrages done to Thee in the course of Thy holy life and bitter Passion. Pardon all the impieties, irreverences, and sacrileges, which have been committed against Thee in the Holy Sacrament of the Eucharist, since its first institution: graciously receive the small tribute of our sincere repentance, as an agreeable offering in Thy sight, and in requital for the benefits we daily receive from Thy altar, where Thou art a living and continual Sacrifice, and in union with that bloody holocaust Thou didst present to Thy eternal Father, on Mount Calvary.

Sweet Jesus! give Thy blessing to the ardent desire we now entertain, and the holy resolution we have taken, of ever loving and adoring Thee, with our whole mind and with our whole heart, in the Sacrament of Thy love; thus to repair, by a true conversion of heart, and a zeal for Thy glory, our past negligence and infidelities. Be Thou, O adorable Heart! Who knowest the clay of which we are formed, be Thou our Mediator with Thy heavenly Father, Whom we have so grievously offended; strengthen our weakness, confirm our resolution, and with Thy charity, humility, meekness, and patience, cover the multitude of our iniquities. Be Thou our Support, our Refuge, and our Strength, that nothing henceforward in life or death may separate us from Thee. Amen.

Act of Reparation for All Consecrated Religious

My Savior Jesus Christ, worthy Victim of the Most High, Thou dwellest in religious houses as in Thine own especial habitation, and amongst the most illustrious portion of Thy flock, in order to make all religious conquests to Thy love, and victims consecrated to Thy glory. This it is which keeps Thee concealed in the tabernacle, and in the enclosure of this monastery, which Thou regardest as Thy chosen vineyard, in which Thou hast raised the stronghold of Thy divine Sacrament, or, in other words, Thine own Body, as an invincible fortress against all its enemies. Thou hast surrounded it with the rampart of the rules and the sublime laws of Thy holy gospel. Thou hast placed there the winepress of Thy adorable Blood, and hast abundantly showered down the heavenly dew of Thy graces over them; and before the whole heavenly court Thou sayest: "What could I do for My vineyard that I have not done to it?" (Is 5:4). I have expected that it should produce good fruit, and it has brought forth only that which is wild and bitter.

O my God, very frequently those for whom Thou hast the most solicitude correspond the least to Thy tenderness, and afflict Thy Heart most profoundly, compelling Thee thus to complain: *Si inimicus meus maledixisset mihi, sustinuissem utique*—"If My enemy had reviled Me, I would willingly have borne with it" (Ps 54:13); but that those whom I have entertained daily at My table, whereof I am Myself the nourishment, should thus rebel—that they, the children of My house, should thus rise against Me—is insupportable to Me. Truly are sins committed in a holy place much more grievous; and it is against such profanations of Thy holy dwellings that Thou hast pronounced this sentence: "He who has done evil in the holy place shall not see the glory of God" (see Is 26:10).

O Lord, let Thy mercy this day arrest the arm of Thy justice; behold me prostrate before Thee in order to make Thee a worthy reparation for all the indignities, tepidity, want of reverence, contempt, and negligence, with which we approach to this adorable Sacrament—for all the Communions made through custom, ostentation, and hypocrisy—for all the sins we commit in this house, which Thou sanctifiest by Thy Real Presence. Ah! I would that my sorrow were great as the sea, that my eyes might shed tears of blood, wherewith to weep over the injuries Thou sufferest from Thy most cherished children, and from myself in particular, who am the most guilty of all. Ah! why have I not enough zeal and fervor that I might worthily repair all the injuries Thou hast received? Vouchsafe to accept these my desires. Would that I could unite in my faith and love, and by the sacrifice I make Thee of whatever is mine, those sentiments with which Thy Holy Spirit has inspired Thy Blessed Mother and Thy saints. Amen.

Act of Reparation to the Agonizing Heart of Jesus

O Jesus, Who lovest souls so ardently, and Who hast endured the most cruel agony to save them, behold us prostrate at Thy feet, to compassionate Thy griefs, and to make reparation to Thine Heart which is outraged daily by the sins of men! O afflicted Heart of our good Master, who can understand the terrors, the anguish, the mortal sadness which oppressed Thee in the Garden of Olives? O sweet Savior of our souls, Thou saidst, "My soul is sorrowful even unto death" (Mt 26:38), and then all our iniquities passed before Thine eyes. It was the sight of those numberless sins which wrung from Thee the doleful complaint: "Father, if it be possible, let this chalice pass from Me" (Mt 26:39). But it covers us with shame and fills us with fresh grief, O heavenly Friend of our souls, to know that we, by our own iniquities, have added to the anguish of Thine agony, and to the torments of Thy death! Oh! Jesus, pardon us! Forget our ingratitude and remember only Thine infinite mercy. Let some drops of the divine blood which watered the Garden of Olives fall upon us, and upon all sinners. Let this adorable blood flow freely, we entreat Thee, down upon the souls of those who are now in the terrible agony of death, and about to appear at Thy death tribunal. O! Jesus, pity them. From the Cross Thou didst pardon the good thief; pardon the dying! Let them also hear from Thy sacred lips the consoling assurance: "This day thou shalt be with Me in paradise" (Lk 23:43).

O! Mary, afflicted Mother, join thy supplications with our humble prayers. Unite thy homage to our expiations, and help us to repair the outrages which we have offered to the agonizing Heart of thy Son Jesus. Blessed archangel Michael, angels of God, faithful guardians of our souls; patron saints who watch over us from heaven, come to our aid. Lend us your holy ardor, that we may adore and love the most amiable and adorable Heart of Jesus; lend us your invincible confidence, that we may obtain, from the infinite clemency of that divine Heart, pardon for ourselves, pardon for our dear country, pardon for all sinners, pardon for the poor dying. O good Jesus, deign to receive, with this reparation, the prayers which we offer to Thee. Bless the members of this pious association, now humbly prostrate before Thee. Kindle anew, and keep alive in their hearts, the sacred fire of Thy divine love, and of zeal for the salvation of souls. Above all, bless the dying. Strengthen them against the terrors of death; defend them against the attacks of the evil spirit. Open to them Thine agonizing Heart for their refuge, and, by its sacred wound, let them enter into the rest of a blessed eternity. Amen.

Let us pray for the associates and companions, living and deceased.

Pater Noster ...

Ave Maria ...

Psalm 129

Out of the depths I have cried to Thee, O Lord: Lord, hear my voice.

Let Thy ears be attentive to the voice of my supplication.

If Thou, O Lord, wilt mark iniquities, Lord, who shall stand it?

For with Thee there is merciful forgiveness: and by reason of Thy law, I have waited for Thee, O Lord.

My soul hath relied on His word: my soul hath hoped in the Lord.

From the morning watch even until night, let Israel hope in the Lord.

Because with the Lord there is mercy; and with Him plentiful redemption.

And He shall redeem Israel from all his iniquities.

Let us pray. O God, the Creator and Redeemer of all the faithful: grant to the souls of Thy servants departed, the remission of all their sins, that by devout supplications, they may obtain that pardon which they have always desired. Who livest and reignest world without end. Amen.

℣. Eternal rest grant unto them, O Lord.
℟. And let perpetual light shine upon them.
℣. May they rest in peace.
℟. Amen.

Quarter-Hour Devotion of Reparation

1. Adore and console Jesus abandoned and despised by men in His Sacrament of love. Man has time for everything except to visit his Lord and his God Who waits for him so patiently and thirsts for His love in the tabernacle. The streets, the theaters are crowded; the house of God, alas! is empty. "O poor Jesus, O neglected Jesus! how canst Thou abide such

indifference from those Thou hast purchased at so great a cost; from Thy friends, from Thy children, from me!"

2. Weep over Jesus betrayed, insulted, mocked, and crucified more cruelly in His Sacrament of love than in the Garden of Olives, in Jerusalem, or on Calvary. And it is too often those whom He has most loved, most honored, and most enriched with His gifts and graces who offend Him most, who dishonor Him most in His holy temple by their irreverence — who crucify Him anew by tepid or even sacrilegious Communions.

O divine Jesus, couldst Thou have believed that the very greatness of Thy love would furnish man with an object for his malice, that he would turn against Thee even Thy most precious gifts and graces!

And I, alas! have I nothing to reproach myself with? Have I ever been negligent or unfaithful to Thee?

3. Adore Jesus, and seek to make reparation for the negligence, profanation, and sacrilege that He meets with so frequently. Offer with this intention all the sufferings that you must endure during the day or the week. Impose upon yourself some penance for your own sins and those of your relations, or for those whom you have disedified by your want of devotion in church, or even by your distractions and levity.

4. But since all your satisfactions and penances are so few and so worthless in reparation for such great sins, unite them with those of Jesus Christ your Savior on the Cross. Gather up the Precious Blood that flows from His sacred wounds and offer it to the divine Justice in reparation. Offer

the prayers and sufferings of the crucified Jesus to the heavenly Father, and beg in return grace and mercy for yourself and all sinners.

Unite your reparation to that of the Blessed Virgin at the foot of the Cross, and you will obtain all that you ask through the love of Jesus for His immaculate Mother.

Act of Reparation to Christ in the Eucharist

Most adorable Savior, by the most wonderful prodigy of Thy love for us, Thou dost shut Thyself up in the most Blessed Sacrament of the Altar, in order to be the perpetual Sacrifice of the New Law, the innocent Victim of our sins, the celestial Food of our souls, our kind Physician, our good Master, our powerful Mediator, and our loving Father. But, alas! With what ingratitude on our part Thine infinite kindness is repaid. Prostrate before Thine altar, where Thou art as really present as in the highest heavens, we come to make reparation for all the injuries and for all the ingratitude inflicted on Thy loving Heart in this Sacrament.

O divine Jesus, grant us to make a fitting reparation for all blasphemies, for all profanations, and all sacrileges ever committed; for the want of devotion and neglect of preparation for Holy Communion, for the little fruit we have drawn from it.

Pardon, O Lord, pardon for so many Christians who know Thee not, and who offend Thee; for so many heretics who insult Thee; for so many impious men and apostates who persecute Thee. By the fervor of our love, we would wish to make amends to Thee for all their contempt, and for all their sacrileges.

How happy should we be, O Jesus, could we but make reparation to Thy glory, by our respect, by our zeal, aye, even by the shedding of our blood. At least, most adorable Savior, grant us the grace to love Thee in the most Holy Sacrament of the Altar, with the most tender, the most generous, the most perfect, the most constant love.

Virgin most holy, by thy holy and Immaculate Heart, make us enter into the adorable Heart of thy divine Son, Jesus Christ.

O sweet St. Joseph! Obtain for me the gift of prayer and of perpetual union with Jesus and Mary. Amen.

Act of Reparation to the Sacred Heart in the Adorable Sacrament

Most amiable and adorable Jesus! always burning with love for us, always sensible of our miseries, always burning with the desire of enriching us with Thy treasures, and of giving Thyself entirely to us! Jesus, my Savior and my God! Thou, Who, through the excess of the most ardent and most extraordinary love, hast deigned to be our Victim in the most adorable Eucharist, in which Thou offerest Thyself daily in sacrifice for us upon thousands of altars! What ought to be our feelings, when we see in the hearts of the greater part of men nothing but forgetfulness, ingratitude, and contempt for Thy favors? Was it not enough for Thee, my dear Savior, to have chosen the most painful of all means to procure our salvation, while it was in Thy power to manifest Thy love in a way which would have cost Thee much less? Was it not enough for Thee to have endured that mortal agony, into which Thou wert plunged at the sight of our sins, of which Thou didst consent to bear the entire weight? Why still expose Thyself to all the indignities which the malice of men and demons inflicts upon Thee? Ah, my God and my Redeemer! what must have been the sentiments of Thy most holy Heart at the sight of so much ingratitude? How great must have been the bitterness which so much insult and sacrilege brought on Thy tender Heart!

Penetrated with the most lively grief at the sight of such ingratitude, behold me prostrate and annihilated in Thy presence, to make Thee, in all humility, a reparation of honor, for all the injuries which Thou hast endured upon our altars since the institution of this adorable Sacrament. With a heart humbled and pierced with sorrow, I earnestly beg of Thee pardon for so much malice. O my God! why can I not wash with my tears, or even with my blood, those places where Thy Heart has been so horribly outraged, and that precious pledge of Thy immense love so little esteemed? Why can I not, by a new sort of homage, of humiliation, of annihilation, repair so many profanations and so much sacrilege? Why can I not even for a moment be master of the hearts of all men; that, by the sacrifice of them, I might repair, in some measure, the negligence and folly of those who desire not to know Thee, or who, having known Thee, love Thee so little? But O my adorable Savior! what covers me with still greater confusion, and still more demands my tears, is that *I* have been of the number of those ungrateful souls. Do then, O Lord, Who knowest my heart, behold the sorrow which I feel for this ingratitude, and the unworthy treatment which Thou receivest from others.

Behold this disposition in which I now am, of doing and suffering everything I can to repair them. Behold me, then, O Lord, with a heart broken with sorrow, humbly prostrate before Thee, and ready to accept from Thy hands whatever Thou pleasest to impose upon me, in satisfaction for all these outrages. Strike, O Lord, strike! I will bless the hand which shall inflict a punishment so deserving. Why am I not a victim worthy to make atonement for so many insults? Why is it not in my power to wash with my blood all those places where Thy sacred Body has been trampled underfoot, and otherwise profaned? Oh, how happy should I be, if, at the price of all possible torments, I were able to atone for so much contempt, so much outrage, so much impiety!

Accept, O eternal Father, this reparation of honor in union with that which was rendered to Thee on Calvary, by the most holy Heart of Thy divine Son, and with that which the most holy Virgin made Thee at the foot of the Cross. Deign to hear the prayer of this divine Heart, pardon me all the indignities and irreverences of which I have been guilty, and, by Thy grace, give efficacy to the resolution which I now form, of never ceasing to love Thee with all the ardor possible, and of ever seeking new opportunities of honoring Thee. O my Sovereign, my Savior, and my God! I believe firmly that Thou art really present in the adorable Eucharist, and I desire in future to testify my belief, by the respect with which I appear in Thy presence, and by my assiduity in adoring Thee. And as I protest that I wish in particular to honor Thy Sacred Heart, contained in the most adorable Sacrament of the Altar, I desire to fix in it my dwelling for the remainder of my life. Grant, O my God, this grace which I beseech of Thee most earnestly, that, at the moment of my death, Thou wouldst receive my last sigh into Thy Sacred Heart. Amen.

Ejaculation to the Sacred Heart[35]

May the Heart of Jesus in the most Blessed Sacrament be praised, adored, and loved with grateful affection, at every moment, in all the tabernacles of the world, even to the end of time. Amen.

Act of Reparation and Consecration to the Sacred Heart

O Sacred Heart of my living Savior, how sensible to our miseries has Thy charity rendered Thee! O my God, what goodness for Thee to place Thyself a Victim for us in the most adorable Eucharist! And yet what dost Thou see in the hearts of the greater part of mankind but rebellion against Thy will and ingratitude for Thy benefits. Was it not enough, O my Jesus, to have abandoned Thyself to a cruel agony in the Garden of Olives, when Thou didst bear the weight of all our sins? Was it not enough to have bought our souls at the price of Thy Blood and Thy death? Was it necessary that Thy ungrateful and perfidious children should dare each day to renew the torments which Thou didst endure in the course of Thy Passion, and, by fresh wounds, to tear open Thy Sacred Heart? Where can we find hearts so hard, that they are not touched at the sight of the outrages inflicted on Thee?

Prostrate and annihilated before Thee, O my Redeemer, permit me this day to make Thee some reparation for all the injuries with which men do not cease to load Thee, and for all the bitterness in which Thy divine Heart is immersed. I wish I could water and purify with my tears all those places where Thou art most offended, and, by my sentiments of burning love, repair the abuse and contempt which is shown of Thy graces by the scandals, profanations, and sacrileges that are committed among Thy children. Would that I had possession of all hearts to offer them to Thee in sacrifice and to console Thee by this homage for the guilty insensibility of those who will not know Thee, or who, knowing Thee, have not loved Thee.

At least, O Lord, I offer Thee myself; immolate me, consume me as Thy victim, grant that I may now begin to love Thee alone, and that after having once consecrated my heart to Thee, I may never take it back again; grant that I may find in Thy Heart an asylum in this world, peace at the hour of death, and my blessedness for all eternity. O Heart of Jesus, mayest Thou be known, praised, adored, and loved by all creatures throughout the universe, now and forever. Amen.

Our Lady of the most Holy Sacrament! Our Lady of the Sacred Heart! Mother and model of adorers, pray for us who have recourse to thee.

St. Joseph, pray for us, that like thee, we may die in the arms of Jesus and Mary.

THE POWER OF REPARATION

Prayer to the Holy Ghost. O Holy Ghost, Thou Teacher and Sanctifier, Who givest light and strength to my soul, bless me that I may be more faithful to Jesus, my Savior and my God, Who is hidden in the Blessed Sacrament, and that I may love Him more and more. In the light of the tabernacle, I ask of Thee, O Holy Spirit, to fill my heart with pure desire for Jesus, the living Bread. Give me grace to adore Him with the zeal and humble veneration of the holy angels; grant that His will may be done on earth as it is in heaven, and that His will be done in my soul. Help me to thank Him for all His gifts, and, most of all, for Himself. By this Holy Sacrament, He strengthens souls on earth, gives rest to souls in purgatory, and gladdens souls in heaven. He is the hidden Manna, promised by Himself to all who overcome themselves and love Him. May I taste the sweetness of Jesus! Set up more and more Thy Kingdom in my soul, that I may keep my body under and bring it to subjection, lest I should be a castaway from Jesus and from Thee.

Spiritual Communion. O Jesus, my Savior, Who art truly present in the Blessed Sacrament for the nourishment of our souls! Since I cannot now receive Thee sacramentally, I humbly and earnestly beseech Thee to refresh me spiritually. I love Thee above all things and I desire to possess Thee within my soul. Come into my mind to illumine it with the light of heaven; come into my heart to enkindle therein the fire of Thy love. Unite me so intimately with Thee, that it may be no more I that live, but Thou that livest and reigneth in me forever.

O Sacrament most holy! O Sacrament divine!

All praise and all thanksgiving be every moment Thine!

Brief Act of Reparation and Consecration to the Sacred Heart

O Sacred Heart of Jesus, my Savior and my God, deign to receive me amongst the number of Thy adorers, notwithstanding my unworthiness. Humbly prostrate in Thy presence, I adore Thee with all the powers of my soul. I consecrate them forever to Thee, with all my thoughts, words, and actions, in grateful acknowledgment for my redemption, but more particularly for Thy love in always dwelling with us, in the most adorable and Blessed Sacrament of the Altar. Oh! why cannot I, O Sacred Heart, by my adorations and those of my associates, repair all the outrages that Thou hast ever received, and will continue to receive until the end of the world, and offer Thee as much love and glory as Thou renderest to Thy eternal Father. Do Thou repair all my faults, be my Protector, my Strength, and my Asylum at the hour of my death.

I petition the like grace for all poor sinners, for all in affliction, for the agonizing, *in fine*, for all mankind, that none may lose the fruits of the Precious Blood Thou shed upon the Cross. May it also be applied for the deliverance of the suffering souls in purgatory; it is what I now request, and will continue to beg until my last breath. Amen.

First Friday Act of Reparation and Consecration

Adorable Heart of Jesus, glowing with love for us, and inflamed with zeal for our salvation: O Heart! ever sensible of our misery and the wretchedness to which our sins have reduced us, infinitely rich in mercy to heal the wounds of our souls, behold us humbly prostrate before Thee to express the sorrow that fills our hearts for the coldness and indifference with which we have so long requited the numberless benefits that Thou hast conferred upon us. With a deep sense of the outrages that have been heaped upon Thee by our sins and the sins of others, we come to make a solemn reparation of honor to Thy most sacred Majesty. It was our sins that overwhelmed Thy Heart with bitterness; it was the weight of our iniquities that pressed down Thy face to the earth in the Garden of Olives, and caused Thee to expire in anguish and agony on the Cross. But now, repenting and sorrowful, we cast ourselves at Thy feet, and implore forgiveness.

Adorable Heart of Jesus, Source of true contrition and ever merciful to the penitent sinner, impart to our hearts the spirit of penance, and give to our eyes a fountain of tears, that we may sincerely bewail our sins now and for the rest of our days. Oh, would that we could blot them out, even with our blood! Pardon them, O Lord, in Thy mercy, and pardon and convert to Thee all that have committed irreverences and sacrileges against Thee in the Sacrament of Thy love, and thus give another proof that Thy mercy is above all Thy works. Divine Jesus, with Thee there are mercy and plentiful redemption, deliver us from our sins, accept the sincere desire we now entertain, and our holy resolution, relying on the assistance of Thy grace, henceforth to be faithful to Thee.

And in order to repair the sins of ingratitude by which we have grieved Thy most tender and loving Heart, we are resolved in the future ever to love and honor Thee in the most adorable Sacrament of the Altar, where Thou art ever present to hear and grant our petitions, and to be the Food and Life of our souls. Be Thou, O compassionate Jesus! our Mediator with Thy heavenly Father Whom we have so grievously offended, strengthen our weakness, confirm these our resolutions of amendment, and as Thy Sacred Heart is our Refuge and our Hope when we have sinned, so may it be the Strength and Support of our repentance, that nothing in life or death may ever again separate us from Thee.

APPENDIX B

ENCYCLICAL ON REPARATION

MISERENTISSIMUS REDEMPTOR
(Pope Pius XI, 1928)

Venerable Brethren:
Health and Apostolic Benediction.

INTRODUCTION

1. Our most merciful Redeemer, having assured the salvation of the human race by His death on the Cross, before He ascended to His heavenly Father, said these consoling words to His sorrowing apostles and disciples: "Behold I am with you all days, even to the consummation of the world" (Mt 28:20). These happy words are also Our own source of hope and salvation, words which, venerable brethren, come readily to mind every time when, from this high watchtower, as it were, We look down upon the human family afflicted by so many grievous ills, and upon the Church, assailed without

respite by attacks and plots. As a matter of fact, this promise of our divine Lord, as it once upon a time raised high the fallen spirits of the apostles and urged them on to spread most zealously the seed of the gospel through all the earth, so also it has guided the Church to victory over the powers of hell. Assuredly, our Lord Jesus Christ has always assisted His Church; and most powerfully and effectively on those very occasions when she was encompassed by the greatest dangers and calamities. Christ then bestowed on her precisely those helps most necessary to meet the conditions of the times, by His wisdom which "reacheth from end to end mightily and ordereth all things sweetly" (Ws 8:1). Nor in our own times has "the hand of the Lord been shortened" (Is 59:1), especially on such occasions when an erroneous doctrine is being taught and spread about throughout the world, and by reason of which we fear that the sources of the Christian life may be dried up, for by such errors men are led to forsake the Christian life and the love of God.

2. Since some Christians, perhaps, are ignorant of, and others are indifferent to, the sorrows which the most loving Jesus revealed to St. Margaret Mary Alacoque in His apparitions to her, as well as His wishes and desires which He manifested to mankind, all of which in the last analysis work to man's advantage, it is Our pleasure, venerable brethren, to write you at some length of the obligation which rests upon all to make those amends which we owe to the most Sacred Heart of Jesus. We feel certain that each of you will zealously teach to your own flocks what We herein write and that you will exhort them to do all that We wish to be done.

Part I: Devotion to the Sacred Heart

Answer to Jansenism

3. From among all the proofs of the infinite goodness of our Savior, none stands out more prominently than the fact that, as the love or the faithful grew cold, He, divine Love itself, gave Himself to us to be honored by a very special devotion and that the rich treasury of the Church was thrown wide open in the interests of that devotion by which we honor the most Sacred Heart of Jesus "in Whom are hid all the treasures of wisdom and knowledge" (Col 2:3). As formerly divine Goodness wished to exhibit to the human race, as it came from the ark of Noe, a sign of the renewed covenant between them, "My bow which appears in the clouds" (Gn 9:14), so in our own so troubled times, while that heresy held sway which is known as Jansenism, the most insidious of all heresies, enemy of the love of God and of filial affection for Him — for this heresy preached that God was not so much to be loved by us as a Father as to be feared as an unrelenting Judge — the most kind Jesus manifested to the nations His Sacred Heart, unfolding our banner of peace and love to the breeze, an augury of certain victory in the battle before us. Wherefore Our predecessor, Leo XIII, admiring as he did the great possibilities which devotion to the most Sacred Heart of Jesus contains, with reason wrote in his Encyclical *Annum Sacrum*: "Just as when the newly-born Church lay helpless under the yoke of the Caesars, there appeared in the heavens a cross, at once the sign and cause of the marvelous victory which was soon to follow, so today behold before our very eyes there appears another

most happy and holy Sign, the most Sacred Heart of Jesus, crowned by a brilliant cross set among raging flames. In this Sacred Heart we should place all our hopes; from it too, we ask and await salvation."

Devotion to the Sacred Heart Praised

4. Are we not to see, venerable brethren, in that blessed Sign and in the devotion which flows from it, the very substance of our holy religion, as well as the rules to guide us toward a more perfect form of life, since the Sacred Heart is the Road which will most surely lead us to know intimately Jesus Christ and will cause our hearts to love more tenderly and to imitate Him more generously than we have heretofore done? Since this is so, it is no wonder then that Our predecessors have always defended this most praiseworthy devotion to the Sacred Heart from the objections launched by those who will not accept it, that they have praised it most highly and have always promoted it with the greatest possible zeal insofar as the conditions of time and place seemed to demand such action. Certainly, it is due to nothing short of the inspiration of God that the childlike love of the faithful for the Sacred Heart increases day by day; that pious associations to promote devotion to the Sacred Heart have come into being everywhere, and that the custom has become quite common of receiving Holy Communion on the first Friday of the month, a custom which had its origin in the wish of Jesus Christ Himself.

Consecration

5. Among the different practices which directly accompany devotion to the most Sacred Heart, assuredly the foremost is the act of consecration by which we offer to the Heart of Jesus both ourselves and all that belongs to us, recognizing that all we have comes to us from the infinite charity of God. Our Lord, having revealed to that most pure lover of His Sacred Heart, St. Margaret Mary, how much more He insisted on the immense love which He has borne toward us than on His rights over us, asked that mankind pay Him this tribute of devotion. Therefore, the saint herself, together with her spiritual director, Claude de la Colombière, first of all offered Him an act of consecration. In the course of time, individuals began paying Him the same tribute, then whole families and certain associations, and last of all, public officials, the inhabitants of cities, and whole nations. Due to the machinations of wicked persons, both in the century just ended and in this century, things had come to such a pass that men despised the rule of Christ and publicly declared war upon His Church by means of laws and popular enactments contrary to both the divine and natural law, even going as far as to cry out publicly: "We will not have this Man reign over us" (Lk 19:14). But, by this act of consecration, there burst forth, in startling contrast to these cries, the unanimous voice of the lovers of the Sacred Heart, rising to vindicate the glory and defend the rights of the same Sacred Heart, "for He must reign" (1 Cor 15:25); "May Thy Kingdom come." Finally, at the beginning of the century, as a happy consequence of all this, the whole human race

which belongs by inherent right to Christ, "in Whom all things are reestablished" (Eph 1:10), was consecrated to His most Sacred Heart by Our predecessor then happily reigning, Leo XIII, amid the applause of the whole Christian world.

FEAST OF CHRIST THE KING INSTITUTED
6. These auspicious and happy beginnings We Ourselves, through the great goodness of God, brought to completion, as was pointed out in Our Encyclical *Quas Primas*, on the occasion when, acceding to the desires and wishes expressed by numerous bishops and the faithful, We instituted at the close of the Jubilee Year the feast of Christ the King of all men, which feast We ordered to be celebrated solemnly all over the Christian world. By that act We not only brought forth clearly into the light of day the fact of the supreme dominion of Christ over all things, over civil society and the home, as well as over individuals; We also experienced beforehand the joy of that most happy day when the whole world will submit joyfully and willingly to the sweet yoke of Christ the King. Wherefore We commanded that, together with the celebration of this feast, there should be renewed annually the act of consecration, and this We did in order to obtain more surely and in greater quantities the fruits of such a consecration and to bind with Christian love in the communion of peace all peoples to the Heart of the King of Kings and Sovereign of Sovereigns.

Part II: Reparation to the Sacred Heart

7. Moreover, to all these expressions of veneration, and especially to that most fruitful one, the act of consecration, which by means of the institution of the feast of Christ the King has been, as it were, again confirmed, it is expedient that another be added, and of this last, venerable brethren, We wish to speak now somewhat at length. We refer to the act of expiation or of reparation, as it is called, to be made to the Sacred Heart of Jesus.

A. Satisfaction for Sin

DUTY OF REPARATION IMPOSED

8. If in the act of consecration the intention to exchange, as it were, for the love of the Creator the love of us creatures stands out most prominently, there follows almost naturally from this another fact, namely, that if this same uncreated love has either been passed over through forgetfulness or saddened by reason of our sins, then we should repair such outrages, no matter in what manner they have occurred. Ordinarily we call this duty, "reparation." If we are held to both these duties for the same reasons, we are held to the duty of making reparation by the most powerful motives of justice and of love: of justice, in order to expiate the injury done God by our sins and to reestablish, by means of penance, the divine order which has been violated; and of love, in order to suffer together with Christ, patient and covered with opprobrium, so that we may bring to Him, insofar as our human weakness permits, some comfort in His sufferings. Since we are all sinners, burdened with many offenses, we should honor

God. This should take place not only by means of that cult by which we adore, in the veneration due Him from us, His Infinite Majesty, or by means of prayer when we recognize His supreme dominion over us, or by acts of thanksgiving when we praise His infinite generosity toward us; it is necessary to do more than all this. We must also satisfy the just anger of God because of "the numberless sins, offenses, and negligences" which we have committed. Therefore, we must add to the act of consecration, by virtue of which we offer ourselves to God and become thereby, as it were, sacred to Him by reason of the sanctity which necessarily flows from an act of consecration, as the Angelic Doctor teaches,[36] an act of expiation, by means of which all our faults are blotted out, lest perchance the sanctity of infinite justice spurn our arrogant unworthiness and look upon our gift as something to be rejected rather than to be accepted.

All men are obliged to make reparation since, according to the teachings of our holy faith, our souls have been disfigured, as a result of the pitiable fall of Adam, by Original Sin; we are subject also to our passions and corrupted in a truly sad way, and have thus made ourselves worthy of eternal damnation. It is true that the proud philosophers of this world deny the above truth, resurrecting in its place the ancient heresy of Pelagius which conceded to human nature a certain inborn goodness which, by our own powers, raises us up to ever higher levels of perfection. These false theories, born of human pride, have been condemned by the apostle who admonishes us that "we were by nature children of wrath" (Eph 2:3). As a matter of fact, from the very Creation of the world, mankind has recognized, in one way or another, the obligation of making reparation, and impelled, as it were, by a natural instinct, has tried to placate the Deity by offering Him public sacrifices.

Christ's Superabundant Satisfaction

9. But no effort on our part would have been great enough to expiate the faults of men if the Son of God had not assumed human nature in order to redeem us. The Savior of mankind announced this truth speaking through the psalmist: "Sacrifice and oblation Thou wouldst not: but a body Thou hast fitted to Me. Holocausts for sin did not please Thee. Then said I: Behold I come" (Heb 10:5–7). In truth, "He hath borne our infirmities and carried our sorrows. He was wounded for our iniquities" (Is 53:4, 5). "Who His own Self bore our sins in His body on the tree" (1 Pt 2:24), "blotting out the handwriting of the decree that was against us, which was contrary to us. And He hath taken the same out of the way, fastening it to the Cross" (Col 2:14), so "that we, being dead to sins, should live to justice" (1 Pt 2:24).

Our Participation in Christ's Sufferings

10. Though the ample Redemption of Christ more than abundantly satisfied for all our offenses (see Col 2:13), nevertheless, by reason of that marvelous disposition of divine Wisdom by which we may complete those "things that are wanting of the sufferings of Christ in our own flesh, for His body, which is the Church" (Col 1:24), we are able to, in fact we should, add to the acts of praise and satisfaction which "Christ in the

name of sinners has presented to God," our own acts of praise and satisfaction. However, we must always remember that the expiatory value of our acts depends solely on the bloody sacrifice of Christ, which is renewed without interruption on our altars in an unbloody manner, since in both cases, "the Victim is the same, the One Who offers Himself by means of the ministry of the priesthood is the same, the very same One Who offered Himself on the Cross, the only difference being in the manner in which the sacrifice is made."[37] For this reason, we must bring together, in the august Sacrifice of the Blessed Eucharist, the act of immolation made by the priest with that of the faithful, so that they, too, may offer themselves up as "a living sacrifice, holy, pleasing unto God" (Rom 12:1). Therefore, St. Cyprian dared to affirm that "the sacrifice of our Lord is not complete as far as our sanctification is concerned unless our offerings and sacrifices correspond to His Passion."[38]

The apostle admonished us that "bearing about in our body the mortification of Jesus" (2 Cor 4:10) and "buried together with Him by baptism unto death" (Rom 6:4), not only should we "crucify our flesh with the vices and concupiscences" (Gal 5:24), "escaping the corruption of that concupiscence which is the world" (2 Pt 1:4), but also that the "life of Jesus be made manifest in our bodies" (2 Cor 4:10), and, having become partakers in His eternal priesthood, we should offer up "gifts and sacrifices for sins" (Heb 5:1). For not only are they partakers in the mysteries of this priesthood and in the duty of offering sacrifices and satisfaction to God, who have been appointed by Jesus Christ the High Priest as the ministers of such sacrifices, to offer God "a clean oblation in every place from the rising of the sun even to the going down" (Mal 1:11), but also those Christians called, and rightly so, by the Prince of the Apostles, "a chosen generation, a kingly priesthood" (1 Pt 2:9), who are to offer sacrifices for sin not only for themselves but for all mankind (see Heb 5:3), and this in much the same way as every priest and "high priest taken from among men is ordained for men in the things that appertain to God" (Heb 5:1).

BENEFITS OF OBLATION AND SACRIFICE

11. In the degree to which our oblation and sacrifice will the more perfectly correspond to the sacrifice of our Lord, that is to say, to the extent to which we have immolated love of self and our passions and crucified our flesh in that mystical crucifixion of which the apostle writes, so much the more plentiful fruits of propitiation and of expiation will we garner for ourselves and for others. A wondrous bond joins all the faithful in Christ, the same bond which unites the Head with the other members of the body, namely, the communion of saints, a bond full of mystery which we believe in as Catholics and by virtue of which individuals and nations are not only united to one another but likewise with the Head itself, "Who is Christ: from Whom the whole body, being compacted and fitly joined together, by what every joint supplieth, according to the operation in the measure of every part, maketh increase of the body, unto the edifying of itself in charity" (Eph 4:15–16). This too was the prayer which Jesus Christ Himself, the Mediator between God and men, at the hour of His death

made to His Father: "I in them and Thou in Me: that they may be made perfect in one" (Jn 17:23).

12. As the act of consecration proclaims and confirms our union with Christ, so the act of expiation, by purifying us from sins, is the beginning of such union; our participation in the sufferings of Christ perfects it, the offering we make to Him of our sacrifices for the welfare of our brethren brings such union to its final consummation. This was precisely the design of the mercy of Jesus when He unveiled to our gaze His Sacred Heart, surrounded by the emblems of His Passion, and aflame with the fire of love, that we, on the one hand, perceiving the infinite malice of sin, and on the other, filled with a knowledge of the infinite love of our Redeemer, might detest more cordially sin and substitute for it an ardent love of Him.

B. Consolation to Christ in His Sufferings

Plea to St. Margaret Mary

13. The spirit of expiation or of reparation has always played one of the chief roles in the devotion of the Sacred Heart of Jesus. Certainly, reparation is most consonant with the origin, nature, efficacy, and particular practices of this special devotion, a fact confirmed by history and the customs of the faithful, by the sacred liturgy, and by the official documents of Roman pontiffs. As a matter of fact, on the occasion when Jesus revealed Himself to St. Margaret Mary, though He then insisted on the immensity of His love, at the same time, with sorrowful mien, He grieved over the great number of horrible outrages heaped upon Him by the ingratitude of mankind. He used then these

words, words, which should be graven on the hearts of all pious souls so as never to be forgotten by them: "Behold this Heart which has loved men so much, which has heaped upon them so many benefits. In exchange for this infinite love, it finds ingratitude; instead, it meets with forgetfulness, indifference, outrages, and all this at times even from souls bound closely to it in the bonds of a very special love."

Communion of Reparation and Holy Hour

14. In order to make reparation for such faults, He, among other requests, made this special request as one which would be most acceptable to Him, namely, that the faithful, inspired by the intention of making reparation, should receive Holy Communion — and for this reason it is called the "Communion of reparation" — and for an hour should practice acts and prayers of reparation before the Blessed Sacrament — which devotion is rightly called the "holy hour." The Church has not only approved these devotions but has enriched them with very special spiritual favors.

How We Can Console Christ

15. But how can we, one may ask, believe that Christ reigns happily in heaven if it is possible to console Him by such acts as those of reparation? We answer it in the language of St. Augustine, words quite apposite to our subject: "The soul which truly loves will comprehend what I say."[39]

Every soul which burns with true love of God, if it but turns its thoughts to the past, sees in meditation and can contemplate Jesus suffering for mankind, afflicted by grief in the midst of sorrows suffered "for us men and for our salvation," weighed down by agony and reproaches, "bruised for our sins" (Is 53:5), in the very act of healing us by His bruises. With so much the more understanding can pious souls meditate upon these mysteries if they appreciate that the sins and crimes of men, no matter when committed, were the real reason why the Son of God was condemned to death, and that even sins committed now would be able of themselves to cause Christ to die a death accompanied by the same sufferings and agonies as His death on the Cross, since every sin must be said to renew in a certain way the Passion of our Lord, "crucifying again to themselves the Son of God and making Him a mockery" (Heb 6:6). And if, in view of our own future sins, foreseen by Him, the soul of Jesus became sad even unto death, there can be no doubt that, by His prevision at the same time of our act of reparation, He was in some way comforted when "there appeared an angel from heaven" (Lk 22:43) to console that Heart of His bowed down with sorrow and anguish.

At the present time, we too, in a marvelous but no less true manner, may and ought to console that Sacred Heart which is being wounded continually by the sins of thoughtless men, since — and we read this also in the sacred liturgy — Christ Himself grieved over the fact that He was abandoned by His friends. For He said, in the words of the psalmist: "My heart hath expected reproach and misery. And I looked for one that would grieve together with Me, but there was none; and for one that would comfort Me, and I found none" (Ps 68:21).

Christ's Passion Renewed in His Mystical Body

16. To the above we may add that the expiatory Passion of Jesus Christ is renewed and in a certain manner continued in His Mystical Body, the Church. To use again the words of St. Augustine, "Christ suffered all that He had to suffer: nothing at all is lacking to the number of His sufferings. Therefore, His sufferings are complete, but in Him as in the Head there remain even now the sufferings of Christ to be endured in the body." In fact, Christ Himself made the same statement, for to Saul, "breathing out threatenings and slaughter against the disciples of the Lord" (Acts 9:1), He said: "I am Jesus Whom thou persecutest" (Acts 9:5). By this He plainly affirmed that persecutions visited on the Church are in reality directed against the Head of the Church. Therefore, Christ, suffering in His Mystical Body, with reason desires to have us as companions in His own acts of expiation, He asks to be united with us, for since we "are the Body of Christ and members of member" (1 Cor 12:27), insofar as the Head suffers so also should the members suffer with it (see 1 Cor 12:26).

C. Need of Reparation Today

Sins in Public Life

17. Now, anyone who uses his eye and mind, if he but think of this world "seated in wickedness" (1 Jn 5:19), can see, as We stated above, how urgent, especially in our own times, is the need of expiation or of reparation. There come to Our ears from every side the cries of nations, whose rulers or governments have actually risen up and have conspired

together against the Lord and against His Church (see Ps 2:2). We have seen both human and divine rights overthrown in these countries, churches destroyed to their very foundations, religious and consecrated virgins driven from their homes, thrown into prison, made to go hungry, treated with unspeakable savagery. We have seen troops of boys and girls, torn from the bosom of holy mother Church, made to deny and blaspheme Christ, and urged to commit the worst sins against purity. We have seen a whole Christian people menaced, oppressed, in constant peril of apostasy from the Faith or of a most barbarous death. These happenings, sorrowful as they are, seem to have been foreseen in such calamities as are now occurring, and to anticipate "the beginning of those sorrows" which will be revealed by "the man of sin who is lifted above all that is called God or that is worshipped" (2 Thes 2:4).

SINS IN PRIVATE LIFE
18. Nor is that other spectacle, venerable brethren, less sad that even among the faithful, washed as they have been by baptism in the blood of the innocent Lamb and enriched by His grace, we encounter so many of every station in life who, ignorant of things divine, are poisoned by false doctrines and live a sinful life far from their Father's house, without the light of the true Faith, without the joy of hope in a future life, deprived of the strength and comfort which come with the spirit of love. Of them one may say quite truthfully that they are immersed in darkness and in the shadow of death. Moreover, disrespect for the discipline of the Church is on

the increase among the faithful as also disrespect for ancient traditions upon which the Christian life has been built, by which domestic society is governed, by which the sanctity of marriage is protected. The process of educating youth has been weakened or spoiled by too much effeminacy, and even the right to educate children in their religion has been taken away from the Church. Christian modesty is forgotten, sad to say, both in our manner of life and of dress, especially by women. There has come into existence, too, an uncontrollable desire to possess the base things of this world, an unreasonable regard for civil interests, an intemperate searching after popular applause, a despisal of legitimate authority and of the Word of God, by all of which the faith itself is shaken to its foundations or placed in jeopardy.

Sins of Apostasy and Sacrilege

19. There must be added to this accumulation of evils the sloth and laziness of those who, like the apostles asleep or like those disciples who had fled away, since they are not firmly rooted in the faith, have shamefully abandoned Christ, burdened with sorrows and attacked by the satellites of Satan, as well as the perfidy of those others who, following in the footsteps of Judas the traitor, either with sacrilegious temerity approach Holy Communion or go over to the camp of the enemy. There thus comes to mind, almost involuntarily, the thought that we have arrived at the hour prophesied by our Lord when He said: "And because iniquity has abounded, the charity of many shall grow cold" (Mt 24:12).

D. Response

INDIVIDUAL REPARATION

20. If the faithful, burning with love for the suffering Christ, should meditate on all these considerations, it would be unthinkable that they should not expiate with greater zeal both their own and the faults of others, that they should not repair the honor of Christ, be filled with zeal for the eternal salvation of souls. Assuredly, we may adapt to our own age to describe it what the apostle wrote: "When sin abounded, grace did more abound" (Rom 5:20), for even though the sinfulness of man has greatly increased, by the grace of the Holy Ghost, there has also increased the number of the faithful who most gladly try to make satisfaction to the divine Heart of Jesus for the numerous injuries heaped on Him. What is more, they joyfully offer themselves to Christ as victims for sin.

Anyone who has been considering in a spirit of love all that has been recalled to his mind up to this, if he has impressed these thoughts, as it were, upon the fleshy tablets of his heart, such a one assuredly cannot but abhor and flee all sin as the greatest of evils. He will also offer himself whole and entire to the Will of God and will strive to repair the injured majesty of God by constant prayer, by voluntary penances, by patient suffering of all those ills which shall befall him; in a word, he will so organize his life that in all things it will be inspired by the spirit of reparation.

GROUP REPARATION

21. From this spirit of reparation there have been born many families of religious men and women, who, day and night,

in tireless manner, have set before themselves the task of taking, in as far as that is possible, the place of the angel who comforted Jesus in the garden. Likewise, certain pious associations, approved by the Holy See and enriched with indulgences, have as their ideal to make reparation for sin by means of certain practices of piety and of the virtues. And not to speak of all these holy works, We select one for mention, namely, the frequent practice of making solemn reparation not only by individuals but often by whole parishes, dioceses, and even nations.

Conclusion

Feast of Reparation

22. Venerable brethren, just as the act of consecration, which began in a small way and afterward came into general use, achieved, by reason of Our approval, the splendid purposes and ends desired, so We wish ardently that this devotion of reparation, which has already been introduced and is the pious custom of certain places, possess the seal of highest approval of Our Apostolic authority, so that it likewise may come to be practiced universally and in a most solemn manner by all Christian peoples. We establish, therefore, and We order that annually, on the feast of the Sacred Heart—which on this occasion We raise to the rank of a double of the first class with an octave—in all the churches of the world, there takes place a solemn act of reparation (the same formula must be used by all and is the one attached to this encyclical [transcribed below]) to our most loving Redeemer, in order that we may, by this act, make

reparation for our own sins and may repair the rights which have been violated of Christ, the King of Kings and our most loving Master.

BLESSINGS EXPECTED
23. Nor can We doubt, venerable brethren, that from this holy practice now reestablished and extended to the whole Church, We may expect many signal blessings, not only for individuals but for society itself, domestic and civil, since Christ Himself promised to St. Margaret Mary that "He would shower abundantly His graces upon those who rendered this honor to the Sacred Heart." Assuredly, sinners "looking on Him Whom they pierced" (Jn 19:37), stricken by the sorrow of the Church, detesting the injuries offered to the King of Kings "will return to themselves" (cf. Is 46:8), for they cannot become obstinate in sin in the presence of Him Whom they have wounded "coming in the clouds of heaven" (Mt 26:64), for then too late and without hope, shall they "bewail themselves to Him" (Apoc 1:7).

But the just will be justified and sanctified still (see Apoc 22:11). They will consecrate themselves with renewed ardor to the service of their King. Seeing Him so despised and so often attacked, seeing too, that so many injuries are inflicted on Him, certainly their zeal for the salvation of souls will be increased when they hear the lament of the divine Victim, "What profit is there in My blood?" (Ps 29:10) and, at the same time, meditate upon the joy of the Sacred Heart "over the sinner who doth penance" (Lk 15:7).

Prayer for God's Mercy

24. We, before all other things, hope and greatly desire that the justice of God, which would have pardoned Sodom if only ten just had been found therein, shall be exercised with more mercy toward all mankind. The faithful in union with Christ, the Mediator and our Head, will pray for and ask from God such mercy. May the most gracious Mother of God be propitious to these Our wishes and to these Our commands; she who gave us Christ the Redeemer, who watched over Him, and, at the foot of the Cross, offered Him a Victim for our sins. She, too, by reason of her wondrous union with Him and of a most singular grace of God, became and is piously known as the Mother of Reparation. Confiding in her intercession with Jesus, "the one Mediator of God and man" (1 Tm 2:5), Who wished to associate His own Mother with Himself as the Advocate of sinners, as the Dispenser and Mediatrix of grace, We impart from Our heart, as an augury of divine favors and a proof of Our fatherly love, to you, venerable brethren, and to all the flock confided to your care, the Apostolic Blessing.

Given at Rome, at St. Peter's, the ninth of May, 1928, the seventh year of Our Pontificate.[40]
PIUS PP. XI

Solemn Act of Reparation

O SWEETEST JESUS, THOU dost pour forth Thy love abundantly on men, while they repay Thee most ungratefully with neglect, indifference, and contempt. Behold us humbly kneeling before Thine altar (outside a church or oratory say: in Thy presence); we would fain repair this heartless ingratitude on the part of men, and the manifold injuries that are everywhere done to Thy most loving Heart, by a special act of homage.

Yet we are not unmindful that we, too, have had our part in this unworthy behavior; therefore are we moved to deep contrition, and, above all, we beg Thy mercy for ourselves; we are ready to atone, by this voluntary act of expiation, for the crimes which we ourselves have committed, as also for the sins of those who, straying far from the way of salvation, either refuse, in the blindness of their unbelief, to follow Thee, the Shepherd and Guide of their souls, or who trample upon the vows of their baptism and shake off the sweet yoke of Thy law.

Not only are we anxious to expiate all these deplorable crimes, but in an especial manner do we purpose to make reparation for these following: immodesty and shameful excesses in life and dress; the many snares of corruption laid for the souls of the innocent; the neglect of holy days; the hateful blasphemies that are hurled against Thee and Thy saints; the reproaches uttered against Thy Vicar on earth and all the priestly order; the neglect, also, of the very Sacrament of Thy love, as well as its profanation by horrifying sacrilege; and finally, the public sins of the nations in rebellion against the just rights and the teaching authority of the Church established by Thee.

Would that we were able to atone for all these outrages even to the shedding of our blood! Meanwhile, in order to atone for the violations of the honor due to Thee, we offer unto Thee that selfsame satisfaction which of old Thou didst offer to the Father upon the holy Cross and which from day to day Thou dost continually renew upon the altars of Thy Church. To this we add the expiatory merits of Thy Virgin Mother, of all Thy saints, and of the devout faithful upon earth. With all our hearts we promise to atone, Thy grace assisting us, for our own past sins and those of all other men, as also for our coldness toward Thine exceeding great love, by a firm faith, spotless purity of life, and the perfect fulfillment, so far as in us lies, of the law of the gospel and in particular of the precept of charity.

We likewise pledge ourselves, in accordance with our strength, to prevent such injuries from being done to Thee, and to invite as many as we can to follow Thee. Accept, we pray Thee, most gracious Jesus, through the intercession of Our Lady of Reparation, this our freewill offering of reparation, and be Thou pleased to keep us, by the great gift of final perseverance, faithful even unto death in our dutiful service of Thee, so that, in the end, we may all come to that our true native land, where Thou, with the Father and the Holy Spirit, livest and reignest forever and ever. Amen.

About the Author

Fr. Raoul Plus, S.J. (1882–1958), wrote more than forty books to help Christians understand God's love for the soul. His works stress the vital role of prayer in the spiritual life and show how you can live the truths of the Faith. A native of France, Fr. Plus studied abroad because of the 1901 laws against religious orders. As a French army chaplain during World War I, he gave the soldiers talks that were to serve as the material for his first two books, *Dieu en nous* (*God within Us*) and *L'Idée reparatrice* (*The Ideal of Reparation*), which were translated into multiple languages. For his wartime services, Fr. Plus was decorated with the *Croix de Guerre*. A renowned preacher and retreat master, Fr. Plus also served as professor of religion and spiritual director at the Université Catholique at Lille and taught at the Institut Catholique in Paris.

Endnotes

1 Every comparison requires some modification. The few drops of water are not required for the validity of the Sacrament, but for its licitness.
2 Conference 66, *De la Réparation*.
3 *Serm. pour la Purif. de la Ste. Vierge.*
4 Philippe Gounard, killed in the war. *Réflexions et Lectures*, pp. 204–205.
5 *Reparation* is commonly used in the sense of compensating *for others*. Clearly this does not exclude the idea of expiating one's own faults when one has committed any, and one's own "indelicacies" which one is never without. We may note an instance of the pain felt by a truly loving spirit at the thought of its least daily shortcomings in the account of *Sister Gertrude Mary* by the Abbé Legueu (p. 99): "I feel quite sad at the thought of loving our dear Lord so little. How grateful I am to you for showing me my indelicacies. *Indelicacy* toward our Lord is a word that touches me very deeply. It has wounded me to the quick. I don't mean, I am annoyed by it. Oh, no: I am very grateful to you for it, but I want to tell you that I feel how much I am constantly grieving our Lord. ... O dear Jesus, in return for all the love Thou dost lavish upon me, I give Thee nothing but indelicacy and ingratitude." After that, we are not surprised at our Lord saying to her: "My child, bestow upon Me numbers of little attentions." (The account is taken from *Une mystique de nos jours* [Angers, 1910].)
6 Msgr. Gauthey, *Vie et Œuvres de la Bienheureuse M.-Marie*, t. 2, p. 425.
7 T. 3, chap. 3. This love does not, however, take away our instinctive horror of pain. Thus we find our Lord saying to St. Teresa: "My daughter, thou askest Me for suffering and then complainest when I send it. ... Nevertheless, I answer thy prayer considering thy set will and purpose, rather than the natural repugnances of thy nature" (*Life of St. Teresa*). Mark well the words *thy will*. It is a question of will and not of feeling. True piety, the piety that

makes reparation, has nothing to do with feeling. This truth should be printed at the foot of every page of this book.

8   Manning.
9   H. Reverdy, *L'absence et le souvenir dans la guerre.*
10 *Folie* in French means "madness" as well as "folly."
11 Perrin, 1903.
12 Robert Vallery-Radot.
13 *Una eademque est hostia, idem nunc offerens sacerdotum ministerio, qui seipsum in cruce obtulit, sola offerendi ratione diversa* (Session 22, "Doctrine on the Sacrifice of the Mass," chap. 2). *In divino hoc sacrificio quod in missa peragitur, idem ille Christus continetur et incruenter immolatur qui in ara crucis semel seipsum cruenter obtulit* (ibid.).
14 See *City of God*, bk. 10, chaps. 6, 21.
15 Grimal, *Le Sacerdoce et le Sacrifice de Jésus Christ*, p. 277 (Beauchesne, 1911).
16 *Méditations sur l'Evangile*: "Cène."
17 Bk. 4, chap. 8.
18 Cf. Augustine, *Confessions*, bk. 8, chap. 11, no. 27.
19 *La Vie Réparatrice* (Desclée, 1909).
20 Vallery-Radot, *Le Vase d'Albâtre.*
21 No one has surpassed Huysmans in expressing these thoughts: "Our Savior cannot now suffer in Person. If He wants to bear suffering on earth, He can only do it through the Church in the members of His Mystical Body. The practicers of reparation, renewing the horrors of Calvary, nailing themselves to the bare blank Cross of Jesus, are after a fashion His counterparts. Nay more, they, and they alone, render to Almighty God something that He lacks, the possibility of continuing to suffer for us. They satiate the desire that survived His death, for it is as infinite as the love from which it springs." They "give the mysterious Needy One the alms of their tears and restore to Him a joy that He has renounced, the joy of being a holocaust" (*Vie de Ste Lidwine*, p. 101).
22 C. 58, § 23.
23 Thomas Aquinas, *Adoro Te Devote.*
24 Leo XIII, May 13, 1903.
25 Pius VII, Rit., August 26, 1814.
26 Pius VII, January 21, 1815.
27 Piux IX, Pr. Ma., September 7, 1854.
28 Pius VII, Res., September 22, 1817.
29 Pius VII, Mem., June 9, 1807.

30 Leo XIII, Br., June 2, 1902.
31 Leo XIII, March 21, 1885.
32 Pius X, March 21, 1905.
33 Pius X, Br., March 29, 1904.
34 Leo XIII, Br., August 16, 1898.
35 Pius IX, February 29, 1868.
36 See *Summa Theologiæ*, II-II, q. 81, a. 1, c.
37 Council of Trent, Session 22, "Doctrine on the Sacrifice of the Mass," chap. 2.
38 Epistle 62, no. 9.
39 *Tractates on the Gospel of John*, Tractate 26, no. 4.
40 Approved English translation of *Miserentissimus Redemptor* taken from Fr. Francis Larkin, *Enthronement of the Sacred Heart of Jesus* (St. Paul: Catechetical Guild Educational Society, 1956), 351–368.

Sophia Institute

Sophia Institute is a nonprofit institution that seeks to nurture the spiritual, moral, and cultural life of souls and to spread the gospel of Christ in conformity with the authentic teachings of the Roman Catholic Church.

Sophia Institute Press fulfills this mission by offering translations, reprints, and new publications that afford readers a rich source of the enduring wisdom of mankind.

Sophia Institute also operates the popular online resource CatholicExchange.com. *Catholic Exchange* provides world news from a Catholic perspective as well as daily devotionals and articles that will help readers to grow in holiness and live a life consistent with the teachings of the Church.

In 2013, Sophia Institute launched Sophia Institute for Teachers to renew and rebuild Catholic culture through service to Catholic education. With the goal of nurturing the spiritual, moral, and cultural life of souls, and an abiding respect for the role and work of teachers, we strive to provide materials and programs that are at once enlightening to the mind and ennobling to the heart; faithful and complete, as well as useful and practical.

Sophia Institute gratefully recognizes the Solidarity Association for preserving and encouraging the growth of our apostolate over the course of many years. Without their generous and timely support, this book would not be in your hands.

www.SophiaInstitute.com
www.CatholicExchange.com
www.SophiaInstituteforTeachers.org

Sophia Institute Press is a registered trademark of Sophia Institute.
Sophia Institute is a tax-exempt institution as defined by the
Internal Revenue Code, Section 501(c)(3). Tax ID 22-2548708.